THE PERPETUAL BEGINNER

A MUSICIAN'S PATH TO LIFELONG LEARNING

DAVE ISAACS

www.NashvilleGuitarGuru.com

ISBN 978-0-57852-083-4
Printed in USA
Cover illustration and book design: Christa Schoenbrodt, Studio Haus

THE PERPETUAL BEGINNER

A MUSICIAN'S PATH TO LIFELONG LEARNING

DAVE ISAACS

CONTENTS

INTRODUCTION

I am thankful every day for music. It has given me a lifetime of joy and solace, diversion and deep meaning, a calling, a vocation, and a place in the world. Most of all, I've come to believe that music provides one of the deepest means of connection between human beings, and a connection to things that words can't adequately express. Many of my strongest lifelong relationships are with current and former bandmates and colleagues, and those shared experiences have made some of my best memories.

If you are reading this, music is probably important to you, too. You may not have chosen to devote yourself to it professionally, but that doesn't diminish its importance in your life. As a hobby, even while playing music might seem to be a mere diversion, it can be deeply meaningful.

One of the most powerful and compelling things about studying music is that the potential for growth is limitless. There's always something new to explore, a technique to improve, a song to learn. Even players who have achieved a level of mastery in one area can set off in a new direction, or push deeper into the frontiers of the territory they know. But this is also part of the challenge to every musician: there's no end to the task, no finish line. Successes can be few and far between, and difficult to measure. The professional has benchmarks to be reached every day, and so can enjoy a sense of accomplishment from the work. But for the more casual amateur, the experience can often feel like a continual struggle marked by occasional victories.

Over 30 years of teaching music, I have worked with students of all ages, levels of skill, and degrees of ambition. Some were (and still are) pursuing a life in music for themselves, but most just want to play. A great many come to me with some experience and knowledge, but they feel that they've reached the limit of what they can accomplish on their own. Some have struggled at a basic level of playing for years, and are frustrated by their seeming inability to improve. Others have acquired many bits and pieces of information, but are still unable to play with fluidity and confidence.

I call these students "perpetual beginners," and I believe they make up a significant percentage of hobbyist musicians. Their goals might vary widely, but what they all have in common is a sense that there's a missing piece of the puzzle. And in fact, there is: while most musicians practice their instrument, far fewer really *practice music*. The technical work of practice is only one aspect of learning to play. The work of developing *musicianship*—overall facility and skill with the language of music—is equally important but often neglected or entirely missed.

I've accumulated a lot of knowledge and experience over my years of playing music, enough to feel that readers would benefit from my sharing it. But despite all that, I can still fall into the same traps that every student faces. Experience raises your baseline level of skill to the point that a pro can "phone it in" and still give a passable performance. But passable performances aren't inspiring to the listener or to the player.

So the title "The Perpetual Beginner" refers as much to me as it might to you. I still have days when I can't seem to make anything connect, and times when I get tired of everything I know how to do. Taking on new challenges or returning to areas where I'm weaker has always broken me out of ruts and stimulated new growth. In other words, a willingness to return to a beginner's mindset has helped me keep my playing dynamic and stimulating.

This is the heart of the message of this book: that experience can lead to stagnation, and that maintaining a beginner's openness and enthusiasm allows you to keep growing for a lifetime. I believe that this and the other insights in this book are the primary reasons I've been able to maintain a life in music, by keeping the love, commitment, and sense of discovery alive.

At the same time, there's no denying that experience builds skill, confidence, and authority. The ideas and tools detailed in the chapters to follow come from the accumulated knowledge of my teachers and mentors, as well as my own years of work as a teacher, writer, coach, and performer. My best teachers understood the power of this combination of "beginner's mind" and the master's skill set. They all shared a passion and lifelong commitment to their craft and art, and showed me what a real life in music might look like. I worked with some of these people for years, but had only a single interaction with others. In every case, I walked away with lessons that still impact my playing and teaching every day.

The goal of this book is to share some of these ideas in a way that will encourage a lifetime of musical exploration. More than helping you to play one thing better today, the most important lessons will teach you how to work at being a better player. What the perpetual beginner needs most is not to learn what else to play, but how to learn.

With such a vast topic as music and musicianship, it's impossible for a single resource to be fully comprehensive. But I've identified some core concepts and skills that I believe are essential for long-term learning. Some are concrete and immediately practical, while others are more philosophical and deal with perspective and motivation. Taken together, these ideas and the interactions they came from have made me into the musician I am today. I hope they will help pave the way for real progress in anyone's musical journey.

This is not a method book or instructional manual. It will not make you a better player overnight, although some of these insights can have an immediate and dramatic impact. My hope is that this book will get you to think differently about what you do as a musician, and give you some tools and skills that will feed your commitment to music for a lifetime.

CHAPTER 1

WHY DO WE PLAY?

CONNECTION, COMMITMENT, AND COMMUNITY

I never thought that much about why I respond to music the way I do. It's something I've taken for granted. After all, music is deeply important to a lot of people, and to some of us it's everything. But in the course of exploring ideas for this book, I began to look more deeply into my own relationship with music, and the reasons why I chose to devote myself to it. Lots of kids wanted to be rock stars, but I knew I wanted a life in music. I made that commitment for the same reason we make lifelong commitments to another person: I fell in love.

ROCK 'N' ROLL FANTASY

Ask many rock musicians why they started playing and you're likely to hear the same answer: it was cool, and a way to be more attractive to the opposite sex. That was absolutely true for me, but I didn't start playing music to meet girls. I started playing music, and fell in love with the guitar.

I'd like to be able to say it started with a flash of inspiration, a bolt from the blue, like seeing Elvis or the Beatles on TV for the first time. But it wasn't that dramatic. I started taking guitar lessons in the spring of 1981 because my mother had insisted that I "do something with myself" the coming summer. I hated the thought of going to summer camp, and lessons were an acceptable alternative to my parents.

I was a typical suburban kid and my taste in pop music at the time was decidedly mainstream: Billy Joel, ELO, Styx, REO Speedwagon. I remember every song on the Billboard Top 100 from 1981. I wasn't really aware of instruments, or who did what on the records I listened to. But I did love music and was consumed by a rush when a song I loved came on the radio. In a superstition that now seems quintessentially early 1980s, I had to have my favorite records on while I played video games. But music was just something I enjoyed, not the obsession it became when I picked up the guitar.

Rock 'n' roll has offered teenagers a chance for a more exciting and dangerous new identity since the 1950s, and I was no exception. Suddenly the music blaring out of boom boxes held by the intimidating denim jacket-clad kids smoking cigarettes at the edge of the schoolyard sounded much more interesting: Led Zeppelin, the Doors, Black Sabbath. My hair grew, my clothes changed, and my imagined path in life changed with it. The guitar was more than a musical instrument to me. It was transformational: a gateway to a thrilling new world, a new social role, and a way to belong.

Of course, the music was plenty compelling on its own, as was the culture that surrounded it. But when it comes to popular music, the two are hard to separate. Every musical movement since the 1920s has been driven by young people's equal desire for excitement and community, from Jazz Age dances to DJ-driven electronic festivals. There's also the element of hero worship and the desire for role models, from Sinatra to Elvis and beyond. The Beatles' first appearance on the Ed Sullivan Show in 1964 (and the screams of the girls in the audience) launched an entire generation of young musicians. Taylor Swift is almost single-handedly responsible for the surge in guitar sales to young women since the mid-2000s.

I continued lessons all through high school, and my crowning moment came at a graduation party when some kids I had jealously watched at a Battle Of The Bands earlier in the year asked me to join in and jam. It was straight out of the movies. I was a shy, shaggy-haired kid, confident in my ability to play but not accustomed to being embraced by the "in crowd." Most of my classmates had never heard me play, and I completely changed in their estimation in the time it took to crank out Van Halen's "Ain't Talkin' Bout Love." Here was the acceptance I had been waiting for since I started playing, and it was sweet.

In retrospect, it seems clear to me that as much as I loved music, I also wanted to become the person I thought being a "guitar player" made me. And I think this is an important reason why I was able to stay with the instrument through the challenging early phase, when so many others lose interest and quit. To a 15-year-old, assuming the role isn't dependent on skill. Playing the guitar made me a guitar player, no matter what I was actually able to do at the time. The social benefits of that role gave me added motivation and sealed my commitment.

Of course, there were other factors at work. Lots of young people take up instruments and join bands to be cool or fit in, and most of them don't pursue careers in music. Talent alone isn't the reason—lots of people have talents they never use or completely fulfill. The identity factor also doesn't work as a motivating force once a person grows into adulthood. But social factors still do.

JOIN THE BAND

Our desire for acceptance and community never goes away, but it does mature. As we come to discover and fully become who we are, what we get from our community changes. Kids need to be accepted and embraced, but adults need to be useful. We find fulfillment in the performance of our role in the group rather than simple acceptance.

As humans, we are often at our best working together in small groups, each member of the team playing their part. Anyone who has ever participated in any kind of group activity with a shared purpose has experienced it: athletes, musicians, actors, or soldiers. When things are at their best, the individuals fade in importance and there is only the well-oiled machine operating as a unit. This is what feels most satisfying to me about playing in a band. The shared experience of the music can create a group consciousness, in which one mind seems to be operating multiple bodies. This collective consciousness lifts everyone's performance to a new level. The whole becomes greater than the sum of its parts.

This "group mind" might be part of what makes us respond to music in the first place. There's a demonstrated correlation between the areas of the brain that respond to music and the areas responsible for social interaction. Most of us have had an experience of collective joy and belonging relating to music, at a religious service, concert, or even a sporting event. It's the reason schools have an alma mater and teams have a fight song. There's an intimacy to this kind of shared experience, even when thousands of people are participating.

As much as I enjoy playing alone, this is why working with others is by far my favorite way to make music. And I believe that it's an essential step in every player's musical life to get into a group of some kind.

You may be perfectly happy as a soloist, and if you have other goals—perhaps to perform, write, or record—they will provide that added push that you need to keep working through the frustrating times. But there's generally a limit to how far you can take things on your own, especially if you don't write or sing. You might even find that you rarely play an entire song!

If no one's singing or listening, you're much less likely to get through the whole thing, unless you're playing along with a recording. And if you don't play full songs regularly, you never develop a sense of the larger flow and *shape* of the song. A piece of music is a sequence of events that unfold and develop. A good performance takes the listener on a journey, but you have to know the whole story to tell it well.

MAKING THE CONNECTION

We all go through periods where we feel like our musical growth has stagnated. But we can rekindle the spark in the relationship and reconnect with the things that made us want to play in the first place. This brings back the enjoyment in playing, and with it the ability to do the work to get better.

If you feel like you've gotten stuck, you may have simply gotten disconnected. Consider the things that motivated you in the beginning. How do those things relate to what you do today? What makes you want to play now, and does your practice or playing time connect you to any of those things? Do you need to reestablish those connections, or make new ones?

There are also several common traps that can lead to frustration, boredom, and ultimately disconnection. See if any of these apply to you.

1. Living on the edge

I had a conversation with an adult student recently who was expressing some frustration with his practicing. He felt like everything he did was a struggle, even though he had developed enough skill to be able to play some of the music he loved.

You might feel that way yourself sometimes. If you do, ask yourself the same thing I asked him: Do you ever play things that are now easy for you? Are you at the edge of your ability every time you pick up your instrument? Or do you play for the enjoyment of playing, too? This is an important part of practicing as well, and one that can be easily overlooked.

Finish every practice session with something you can play well. It's important to work on things that challenge you, but it's equally important to feed the love.

2. Playing notes instead of music

There's more to playing musically than just hitting the right notes. Flow, feel, and vibe are more subtle things that come with time, attention, and experience. You have to be able to play the song comfortably in order to really "get" these subtleties. This is why revisiting familiar music is so important: there's almost always something more to be learned or explored. It might be a subtlety of the rhythm, being able to execute a part more naturally, or even just remembering the words from top to bottom.

These finer points of performance are what make music compelling to the listener *and* the player. Finding and

7

practicing those nuances can really breathe new life into your practice sessions, as you discover new elements in songs you thought you already knew.

3. Going it alone

Most non-professionals (and some pros) spend most of their time playing alone. We've already looked at some of the problems this presents. From a practical standpoint, there are skills and a level of confidence that I don't believe you can reach without playing with and for others. But even more importantly, you miss out on possibly the best part of making music: the connection.

Whether you're performing solo and connecting to the audience, or playing in a group and wordlessly communicating with the other players, the experience is deeply satisfying. In addition, performances and jam sessions create a compelling reason to play and practice by setting concrete goals and deadlines. But the social aspect of making music together is more than enough motivation in itself.

It may take some initiative to find the right setting, but most communities have some kind of open mic night at a club or neighborhood coffeehouse. Many community music schools offer band classes; this can also be a place to look for other players like you. And classifieds aren't just for pros, as any glance at Craigslist will tell you. Be creative—there are all kinds of ways to find musicians and an audience.

After over 30 years of playing professionally, I still need to play and perform. I become restless and unhappy if I don't. I've developed enough skill that I can comfortably enjoy playing a wide variety of music. But the social aspect of music-making remains the strongest driving force for me. I am happiest when playing with others, and especially when that playing becomes a dynamic conversation in which I am an easy participant. At its heart, music is about connection: an emotional connection to people and events, a physical connection to the experience of playing, and a social connection to the rest of the world. These are the things that keep me motivated and inspired today, and it can be the same for you.

CHAPTER 2

THE TALENT TRAP

IT'S WHAT YOU LEARN,
NOT WHAT YOU WERE GIVEN

People didn't used to worry about whether they had a gift for music. It was a part of everyone's life in some way. Families and communities sang together, and often played music together. There were always some with more ability than others, but participation was a part of the culture and not dependent on a person's perceived level of "talent" the way it is today.

There's no disputing that talent exists, but its significance is misunderstood. It's most helpful to think of what we call "talent" as natural ease and facility, both physical and mental. Even in athletics, ability has as much to do with the mind as with the body: depth perception, spatial intelligence, and strategy are all essential to great athletic performance, as is the mental focus that intense training demands. Talent can be seen as the intersection between strength in a particular area of awareness and the requirements of a particular skill. This manifests as natural ability, and at its best we call it genius.

Of course, there's more to becoming a confident player than simply having a gift. Every unschooled "natural" player I've ever met still had to put in many hours with the instrument. The natural part of this ability is how these players absorb information intuitively, often by imitation alone. But it's difficult to quantify just what is intuitive versus what is consciously observed or taught.

There's no way of knowing just how much of a great player's ability was given and how much has been earned, but you can be sure that more was probably earned than you think. When people say, "He never took lessons," it doesn't mean that person didn't have to learn anything, or didn't have to work to do it.

Talent helps, but there is a lot more to the complete picture. That should be encouraging to readers who feel like they don't have it! And the perception that you do have talent can lead to its own challenges.

TWO TRAPS

There are two major "traps" that our perception of talent might create. One is that those who feel they don't "have it" question whether they'll ever be able to play. For those that clearly do "have it," natural ability can make it more difficult to do the hard work when it's required.

The musical intuitive can proceed by instinct up to a

certain point, but eventually conscious knowledge has to come into play. Some are so naturally gifted that they reach a very high degree of skill and success before that happens, and some of your musical heroes likely fall into that category. But most people are somewhere along the vast spectrum between ignorance and genius, and we don't know where our personal ceiling is until we hit it.

Sometimes those with greater gifts find it even more challenging to break through that ceiling because they have never needed to work at music before. It's frustrating to find yourself struggling when you've always been confident. Once we find a place that feels good, we tend to not want to leave it—wherever that happens to be. But this applies to everyone regardless of talent. It's possibly the main reason why people stop improving.

If you take a moment to think about the question of talent, you just might come to realize that the answer is irrelevant. What looks like talent alone is also a product of effort and experience. Talent might grease the wheels, but everyone still needs to pedal the bike uphill. So the question of whether you or anyone else has the talent to learn to play is pointless. Even worse, it might very possibly stop you from making the effort to really improve, whether the answer is yes or no.

NATURAL ABILITY AND ACQUIRED SKILL

No one looks at natural ability as a prerequisite for

enjoyment in athletics. The benefits of sport of any kind for the mind and body are well known and the world is full of happily unskilled amateurs. But when it comes to music, we seem to believe that only the best should participate.

I worked for many years as a neighborhood music teacher, teaching primarily children. Some of these kids had a real desire to play, while others were casual at best. But unless they were clearly excelling, at some point I would be asked whether the child "had any talent." It always seemed to me that the question I was really being asked was whether the parents were wasting their money paying for music lessons!

My answer was always the same: that everyone has the potential to learn to make music in some way. I think every teacher's role is to find a way to make that happen, not to judge whether or not it's worth the effort. The fact that the question would be asked at all is a symptom of a larger issue in our culture when it comes to music—one that presents a particular problem to the perpetual beginner. We've come to see music as a spectator sport rather than a participatory one.

Our kids play music in band or orchestra in school, and many take lessons and go to summer music camps. But by the time they reach college or shortly thereafter, most have given up. In some ways, it's just a practical matter of time and opportunity: if you played in the sixth grade band, you had a dedicated time and place for practice, regular guidance, and built-in goals to work towards. This kind of dedicated structure is important, and much harder to maintain later in life. But there's also an underlying belief, sometimes expressed more directly and sometimes unspoken, that continuing to play is only worthwhile if you're going to "do something" with it.

It's generally true that those who are gifted are the ones that go on to pursue careers in music. Their predisposition allows them to progress faster and achieve the satisfaction of playing well much sooner. This leads more easily to the kind of devotion that a life in music demands. The devoted, skilled amateur is more rare—partly because struggling is frustrating, and partly because many people believe deep down that they just don't "have it."

But we can easily quantify the skills that making music requires, along with the means and methods to learn them. A natural affinity helps, but ultimately all of these skills are teachable. There's a difference between lacking a predisposition and lacking the ability to learn at all. Not everyone is going to become highly skilled, but learning to play relies on many more factors than natural ability alone. And one of the most important has more to do with a simple decision than with any natural gift: the decision to start listening.

CRITICAL LISTENING

Listening is the most important skill a musician needs to develop. It's the most important way we learn music, both consciously and unconsciously. And while some people are born with a more precise ear than others, everyone's ear can be educated.

"Critical listening" is at the core of the distinction between listening and hearing, the difference between how trained and untrained ears perceive music. Some of that training might be formal, and some might be more intuitive—here's where talent and predisposition come in. But by using the word "critical," we make a distinction between what we might call *active* and *passive* hearing. This is a conscious choice musicians make between simply enjoying music and learning something about it as they do.

Active hearing means that the listener comprehends the relationships they hear, either analytically (to the formally schooled) or intuitively (to the unschooled). A skilled musician can listen to music and be able to reproduce the sounds by translating the sonic relationships to physical ones on the instrument. The most gifted natural musicians do this easily, without any need to categorize or label what they hear. They can eliminate the middle steps, like mathematical savants who can effortlessly solve equations in their heads. In some ways, that's exactly what it is. And just as anyone can be taught the concrete steps to solve an equation—every high school math curriculum expects us to learn this as a matter of course—anyone can also learn to hear the discrete elements in a piece of music.

One of the first records I became obsessed with was a Beatles compilation of their recordings from the later half of the band's career. These were the experimental years after they had stopped touring, fueled by musical curiosity and more than a little LSD. So the sounds are wildly diverse and creative: the mellotron opening of "Strawberry Fields Forever," and the wildly chaotic orchestra crescendo in "A Day in the Life." But I was completely unaware of the source of any of these sounds, and I never even thought to wonder what they were. Many of them I didn't even notice. I remember the first time I heard the clarinet counterpoint in the chorus of "Ob-La-Di, Ob-La-Da," even though I had already listened to the song a hundred times.

I think that's typical. Most people listen to a song and hear only the vocal against a collective sound that they are only dimly aware of. But when we start to listen critically, the different parts start to reveal themselves. I've heard many people relate this anecdotally, and seen it over and over working with students. I've also experienced the process repeatedly with the same music as I came to understand more and more.

We've heard music all our lives, but most people have never thought to listen more closely than simple enjoyment requires. I'm convinced that almost everyone can become more attuned to musical detail by simply paying attention. When you do start listening more closely, a deeper understanding starts to emerge. At the heart of this understanding is the recognition that music comes from relationships between sounds.

"PERFECT PITCH" AND RELATIVE RELATIONSHIPS

The skill we call "perfect pitch"—the ability to name notes by hearing them—is a perfect example of a latent skill, something most people believe you have to be born with. All music is vibration, and different notes vibrate at different speeds or frequencies, measured in cycles per second (hertz, abbreviated Hz). So there's a physical element to every note, and sensitive ears will be particularly attuned to the difference between them, just as a sharp eye can easily measure distance. But in either case, you still have to learn what "A" sounds like (or how far 100 yards is) and associate that note name with the sound and feeling that the particular frequency creates. The difference isn't in the ability to learn but in the ease of learning. This is important to recognize, because if you believe you need to have a skill from birth, it's unlikely you'll ever try to develop it.

However, the ability to recognize musical *relationships* by ear is more important to the musician than the ability to name individual notes. A song performed in different keys is clearly the same song, but the different key creates a different feeling. We recognize the melody because of the familiar *interval* pattern, the distance from one note to the next as the music progresses. Familiar tunes are often used as tools in ear-training classes as a reference for recognizing specific intervals: "Here Comes the Bride" for a perfect fourth, or the opening notes of the theme from "Star Wars" for a perfect fifth. We learn to recognize the sound by its association with something else. The same goes for chord sequences and harmony: repeated close listening, combined with some kind of reference, develops the ability to differentiate between patterns and qualities of sound.

Mastering this ongoing process comes with experience, not latent talent alone. I had enough of an ear that I could pick out simple melodies as a child, but compared to many musicians I've known, my gifts were pretty modest. Most of what I know as a musician was learned, and most of that came from learning to listen critically.

PRACTICAL EAR TRAINING: CLASSIFYING SOUNDS

Ear training begins with differentiating and classifying sounds. Most people have never made an effort to do this. In my experience, most begin to hear differently almost right away. Something as simple as identifying a beat can be an unfolding process, like peeling away layers. Stay with me and let's take a closer look.

Musical relationships are hierarchies, with primary, secondary, and even tertiary elements. Looking at rhythm, we might work our way outward like this:

1. Pulse: steady beat
2. Meter: how those sounds line up on a cyclical timeline
3. Specific rhythm: when sounds happen relative to the cyclical beat

We can break down melody like this:

1. Activity and duration: how often we hear new sounds, and how long each one lasts
2. Rhythm: when the notes happen, relative to the timeline established by the pulse and meter
3. Line and contour: whether the notes move up or down, and in large or small increments

Harmony also breaks down into individual elements:

1. Harmonic rhythm: when the chords change relative to the timeline
2. Relationships between chords: for example, a common chord progression or sequence
3. Specific chords built on specific notes

There are other overlapping relationships as well, such as the relationship of melody and harmony. You may not have ever thought about music in such specific and discrete terms, but when you do, you're likely to find that you can focus on the different elements individually. You may not perceive them in this order, and you might hear more than one at the same time. But just as effective practicing often depends on isolating specific musical elements, it's often easier to hear specific things one at a time. (See Chapter 3, "On Practicing," for more details about practicing these elements of music.)

Translating the sounds to your instrument can be more challenging. The process can be purely trial and error, and may require many repeated listening sessions. I find that there are things I can hear right away and others that I won't even notice until I've listened many times over. It's gotten easier over the years, because my ability to differentiate and classify sounds has continued to grow with experience, even after my formal schooling ended. Informal schooling, of course, never ends—at least, as long as we remain open to it.

Ten steps, from concepts to confidence:

1. Talent is a practical advantage, but not a requirement.
2. All accomplished musicians have been "educated" in one way or another.
3. The elements of music can be quantified and learned.
4. Some learn more easily than others, but everyone is capable.
5. The most important lesson is learning to listen.
6. Critical listening allows the musician to recognize and classify sounds.
7. The information gathered through critical listening creates a musical vocabulary.
8. Familiar songs provide examples of how that

vocabulary can be used.

9. Experimenting with that vocabulary builds confidence.

10. Now go play!

CHAPTER 3

ON PRACTICING

THE IMPORTANCE
OF METHOD
AND RITUAL

One of the great luxuries of being a music student was having time to practice. It didn't feel like a luxury to me at the time though. In moments of frustration, it felt more like the need to practice was a life sentence I had consigned myself to.

As a classical guitar student I generally had a solid hour-long program of solo guitar music to prepare for performance. This alone required two to three hours minimum to practice thoroughly. There was also ensemble music: guitar ensemble, duets with flute, violin, or another guitar, and the occasional larger-scale piece. In addition, I had a warm-up regimen to work through each day before I played a note of concert repertoire.

A music student's lifestyle is meant to be conducive to this kind of practicing, but available time, pressure, and sheer discipline weren't the only factors at work. I was able to maintain a routine because it was a ritual, a regular and enjoyable part of my day.

It's not likely that you're managing the same amount of material or working quite as intensely. But the strategies that helped my practice regimen to become a regular part of my day can also help you organize and make the most of your own practice time.

ECHOES IN THE HALL

The music department at Queens College of the City University of New York was in Rathaus Hall, pronounced "rat house," which I found endlessly amusing and somewhat appropriate. Some college buildings are marvels of architecture, but this one was not: it was an unlovely, solidly functional rectangle of white brick, cinder blocks and concrete with rows of windows. At one end, the entry and stairwell formed a separate square that rose half a floor above the rest of the building. At the other, a warren of tunnels connected to the backstage area of the Colden Auditorium next door.

The cinder block walls and concrete steps of the stairwell created a dramatic natural reverb, so the landing above the second floor was a favorite spot to practice. I would come in well before class and set up at the top of the stairs to go through my technical sequence, which lasted about an hour. The sound of the guitar echoing through the stairwell was very satisfying, and added a lot to my enjoyment of a routine that might have been tedious otherwise.

When I describe my practice to my students now, they are often amazed at how simply I would begin: just playing open strings. But it was very satisfying to sit down with my morning coffee in a familiar environment and just listen to the sound of the guitar echoing through the space. The fact that my mind wasn't fully active yet helped maintain the focus on simple things. As I worked my way through my coffee, I gradually worked my way into the day's relationship with the guitar, progressing from open strings to simple arpeggios, scales, finger exercises, and finally musical etudes.

I've found similar spots for practicing over the course of my musical life. Having a dedicated place, especially at a regular time of day, makes it easier to get into a working mindset. Many writers say much the same thing. As I work on this book, I have a favorite table at my office where I sit and write in the mornings before I start teaching. I've also heard people say the same thing about yoga practice. Repeating a task or practice in a particular place seems to infuse that place with the right energy, especially if it's the only thing you do there.

GETTING ORGANIZED

Learning how to practice is one of the most important lessons you can learn as a musician. For the beginner, practicing is mostly pure repetition. To some extent, that's always going to be true, and most great musicians spent many hours with their instrument when they were young and had all the time in the world. At some point, though, that honeymoon ends and the need for efficiency takes over. Professionals have a limited amount of time to learn and perfect a performance. So one of the skills a pro must develop is the ability to practice effectively: to maximize the impact of the time spent.

There are various kinds of practice to accomplish different goals:

- Pure technical practice for skill development
- Targeted problem-solving practice within a specific piece of music
- Learning new vocabulary on the instrument and by ear
- Learning and performing a specific repertoire

The technical element is always present in some way. You might practice a particular technique the way it appears in a specific song. Problem-solving practice is almost always technical in nature, in that every mechanical problem has a mechanical solution. And learning new vocabulary has its technical elements as well.

We can also think of dividing practice time into two kinds of work: micro and macro. "Micro" practice improves the execution of a specific thing: a note, chord, or passage. "Macro" practice improves the overall performance. An effective practice session incorporates both, starting with a laser focus on the micro details and working outward to incorporate them into the bigger picture.

TAKING AIM

I often ask a new student if they have any particular goals, and the answer is usually that they want to be able to play better. But that part goes without saying. People look for guidance because they need help in setting goals, not just reaching them. Once established, your goal provides a clear target.

These goals can be arbitrary; there doesn't have to be a compelling reason to choose one over another. But their reason for being is compelling: to compel you to work on a specific thing hard enough to make it happen.

Your goal might be as modest as wanting to be able to play one song confidently onstage, or as ambitious as you can imagine. It might involve a particular event, a specific skill set or repertoire, or something open-ended, like starting a band or writing songs. Regardless, your goals provide motivation and accountability, as well as some of the details you'll need to know to reach them. Those details will determine what your practice routine looks like. It's impossible to hit a target you can't see—so clarify what you want to accomplish and take aim.

Some of your "micro" practice might remain devoted to more general skill development, especially as you establish a routine. There's a lot to be said for this kind of organized work if you can maintain your focus and discipline. The technical routine I practiced with my morning coffee as a student was like this. The goals that drove the rest of my "macro" practice in those days were performance-oriented, usually working up a piece for a specific concert. Time spent in micro practice was also devoted to problem-solving within the music chosen for the macro goals.

Professional concert recitalists continue to do this, choosing a program of material well in advance of their performance and then devoting practice time to preparing it. Bands do the same thing in a different way. They focus on their most recent material or, in the case of a legacy act, choose a set list that covers a cross-section of their career. In some cases, "practice" just means choosing the songs and running through them to refresh the players' memories. In others, practice will require detailed work to put the pieces together.

CHOOSING A REPERTOIRE

A good place to begin is to assess where you are. If you've been playing music for any length of time, you've almost certainly developed a repertoire, a set of songs or pieces that you've learned to play. Make a list of these, if you don't have one already. Try to catalog them according to how well you can play them. Odds are that the songs will be in different stages of development, and you'll be more proficient with some than with others.

Ideally, over time the amount of music in the "proficient" column should steadily grow, but many people find that it doesn't. It's very common to start working on something, develop it to a certain point, and then put it aside before you really absorb it. Without a compelling reason to keep working, it's easy to get frustrated or lose interest. This is possibly the single biggest trap for the perpetual beginner, and the reason why setting concrete goals is so important.

Once you've established the music you want to be able to play, you can start structuring your practice time to address the things that need attention. On the micro level, this will involve the first two of the four types of practice we've established earlier in this chapter: overall technique and specific problem-solving within a particular song.

You will probably find that all your technical challenges fall into one of two categories. The problem is either mental—that is, a lack of clarity or attention to detail—or mechanical, usually a result of a breakdown in coordination and control. Often, it's a mix of both: a lack of clarity hiding a technical limitation. Either way, details that were previously fuzzy or even unnoticed will become crystal clear when you really start to pay attention.

FOCUS

Once you understand the primary issues, focus your practice on one specific element at a time. My morning coffee warm-up started with plucking open strings, the most basic thing you can do on a guitar. It might sound absurdly simple, but consider the variables. If you're plucking with the bare fingers, there's the question of which finger or combination of fingers to use. Then each finger has to produce a consistent, uniform sound. Slight variations in attack will produce slightly different tones. That's a lot to think about for such a simple exercise!

So the practice sequence would start with the most basic moves and then add other musical elements in different combinations:

1. Repeated notes with the same finger, matching tone and attack
2. Alternating fingers on the same string in different combinations, playing "bursts" of 2, 3, 4, 5, and 6 notes
3. Alternating fingers, crossing strings
4. Adding held chords in the fretting hand
5. Arpeggio figures: patterns across the strings while holding a chord
6. Short scale segments, crossing strings
7. Complete scales
8. Scales with repeated notes (for example, CCCC DDDD EEEE, etc.)

All the while, each exercise is broken down to the simple components in each hand: the finger or pick striking

the string, and the fretting-hand fingers landin
neck, all executed smoothly and in sync. It take
concentration.

Most people don't think to break things down this far,
and not every situation requires it. Some people are naturally fluid and play with more ease than others. Some
things are just easier to play. But if you find that you consistently struggle with something, you probably need to
get out the microscope and take a much closer look.

You are probably not putting in three to five hours a
day of organized practice, and the music you want to play
might not be as demanding. But the technique of identifying and isolating specific elements or issues can be applied
to everything we do in music. It's a problem-solving method you can use for anything you might be working on.

SLOW DOWN!

The single biggest issue most people have is playing too fast
when they practice. It's actually harder to practice slowly,
because it's mentally more taxing to keep track of where
you are. For slow practice to be effective, it has to bypass
muscle memory so that every movement is intentional and
deliberate. This is hard work and sometimes tedious—but
think of it as controlled and detailed rather than slow and
boring! In fact, if you find you're bored, there's a good chance
you aren't paying attention.

There is so much to think about in the mechanics alone:

the right notes with the right fingering, good tone, efficient technique, and proper timing. When those are firmly in place, add in the musical elements of phrasing, articulation, and dynamics. It's important to recognize how much of your ability to play well comes from your detailed attention to *all* of these elements. Anything less is faking it, and the result is that a good performance becomes much more dependent on chance than skill.

The metronome is your friend and taskmaster when you are practicing so slowly. I had a teacher refer to its maddening regularity as "the tyranny of the steady beat," and thought of this often when I found myself struggling. The metronome is a valuable tool, though. It became much more fun to use when I learned something fundamental about rhythm: there's more to having "good time" than the ability to keep a steady tempo.

UNDERSTANDING RHYTHM

We often think about timing in terms of *tempo*. This is the pace of the music, measured in beats per minute, and starts with the most basic aspect of rhythm: the pulse.

Almost all music has a pulse, as do most living things. After all, nature is rhythmic. Celestial bodies move in time at predictable intervals. Waves crash on beaches, insects buzz in the trees, and hearts beat. Machines have a pulse: clocks, motors, spinning wheels. A rhythmic pulse organizes sound into music, and playing well at any tempo depends on it. However, that pulse is more flexible than you might think, even when you're playing to the mechanical click of a metronome.

Pulses can be grouped into regular cycles to create *me-ter*, a pattern of stronger and weaker beats. Even working with a metronome, you can organize the pulse by simply counting beats: one, two, one, two. Notice how this creates movement—an alternation between two poles, like a swinging pendulum. Old-fashioned mechanical metronomes had a physical weight that swung back and forth, adding a useful visual element. The metronome also establishes a rhythmic hierarchy, with the first count of every cycle receiving subtle emphasis, even if you don't add a conscious accent.

Pulses can also be subdivided into twos, threes, fours, or even further. The "feel" of any piece of music comes from the way that steady pulse is grouped into meter and subdivided into specific rhythms. You can use this insight to help you keep time and to give any exercise a more musical feeling, no matter how simple it is.

Let's say you're practicing a passage at half-speed. Cutting the pulse in half can make it harder to keep time, because the slower tempo is hard to measure out and the music doesn't feel like it's supposed to. But what if you keep the same pulse and just count it differently? If your goal is to play quarter notes (one note per beat) at 100 beats per minute, half speed would be 50. Rather than slowing the metronome down that much, try counting each beat of the metronome as if it were an eighth note: "1 and 2 and." In effect, you've cut the tempo in half, but kept the same pulse. Hearing the eighth note makes it easier to stay in time, and it also reinforces your ability to hear and feel *offbeats*, the beats that fall between the counts.

Try this at a variety of tempos, making sure you can maintain your accuracy as you speed up. The fastest tempo you can maintain without mistakes is what we would call your "ceiling." Identifying where that ceiling is will allow you to work on building real speed and control.

THE CONDUCTOR

Big-picture "macro" practicing begins with musical rather than technical questions. In macro practicing, your focus is on flow: your ability to perform the music confidently and communicate the feeling that you want. Technique is always a part of the equation, because every musical gesture has a technical foundation. Our fine-tuning work is meant to eliminate obstacles to the flow so you can focus on expression rather than mechanics. This puts the spotlight on subtleties of tone, phrasing, and dynamics, while allowing you to feel the flow of song as a whole.

Working in this way requires practicing gestures instead of notes. Rather than working on discrete elements one at a time, this kind of practice is like conducting an orchestra: managing a collection of musical elements that interact in real time. This analogy should clarify the "gesture" concept: think of the conductor's movements as the music swells in volume, or changes from one feeling to another. The individual musicians are focused on their parts, but the conductor directs the collective whole.

In a popular music context, the analogy still works. A solo performer is band and bandleader all at once, balancing harmony, rhythm, and melody. In a group setting, macro practice allows the players to get to know each other's parts so that the ensemble can interact, really playing *together* instead of all at the same time. In either case, the goal of this kind of practice is to control the dynamic and rhythmic balance among all the elements, while shaping individual melodic lines—all at once! It's a complicated dance that some can perform intuitively, but even so, repeated practice makes the process fluid and authoritative.

ORGANIZING YOUR PRACTICE ROUTINE

1. Evaluate your goals. Find the thing that will give you a reason to do the work.
2. Evaluate your existing repertoire to see if it serves your goals. Determine what type of practice each song needs.
3. Establish a time and place that will allow you to make practice a ritual. Develop a sequence that strengthens your relationship with your instrument each day while serving your larger goals.
4. Allow time for regular micro and macro

practice. If one becomes frustrating, switch to the other. Be patient and give things time to progress—but also rotate your material to help you maintain freshness and enthusiasm.

It can be helpful to seek out the direction of a more experienced player and teacher to help you evaluate your skills, needs, and the effectiveness of your practice routine. At the same time, remember that one of your most important goals should be to develop the ability to self-diagnose: to evaluate and teach yourself. Organizing your practice in a coherent, mindful way is an important step in that direction.

CHAPTER 4

INSTRUMENT & BODY

CREATING A MENTAL MAP

Great musicians make playing their instruments look as natural as breathing. They play with it: sometimes dancing with it, sometimes seeming to make it a part of them.

If you've ever struggled to get physically comfortable while you practice, you might feel like you'll never be that fluid. Some people are always uncomfortable and don't even realize it, only knowing that they can't play the way they'd like. Ultimately, most people don't give much thought to their physical relationship with their instrument. As long as it feels like a foreign object, you're likely to struggle. But when it feels like an intimate friend, making music becomes effortless.

In this chapter, we'll introduce the concept of "body mapping," and get you to explore the way you relate to your instrument. It's an ongoing process, and one you may never fully master; it's impossible to be completely tuned-in all the time. But you can get in the habit of paying attention

FEELING THE BODY IN SPACE

Musicians can use their bodies as intensely as athletes do. The parallel isn't in the sense of pushing the body's limits, but in performing a specific series of movements with great control and precision. Watch a great pianist's fingers dance across a keyboard with the lightness of an Olympic gymnast. Most of the activity might be in the hands, but in that small area of the body, the demands are just as great.

This can lead to a trap that's particularly challenging for pianists and string players, or anything that's hand-intensive: when we are hyper-focused on the fingers, it's easy for the rest of the body to disappear.

Athletes, dancers, and yoga practitioners understand the concept of a mental "map" of the body, an awareness of the body and its position in space. Musicians are taught to think about general posture and efficiency of movement, but they may not often consider the body as a whole. A mental map allows you to keep track of the way any movement affects the rest of the body. Imagine a ballet dancer's hands: they might not be central to the movement being performed, but the dancer is still aware of their position relative to the point of balance at the center of the body. In other words, the mental map encompasses the entire body, not just where the activity is.

Try this simple visualization exercise:

1. Sit in a straight-backed chair and pay attention to three points of contact: your two feet on the floor and your seat on the chair. Imagine this as an offset tripod or a triangle.
2. Sit up straight and imagine the line of your spine rising from your pelvis to the top of your head. Visualize your head floating on top of your spine, which hangs down like a string from a helium balloon.
3. Let your shoulders drop back and down. Imagine a triangle formed by the shoulders and the top of the head, and another formed by the shoulders and the base of the spine. Visualize the upper body as a pair of opposing triangles balancing on top of a tripod base. Explore this idea of balance. Don't force your breathing or strain to sit up, just float. Feel the helium balloon that is your head gently rise and lengthen the spine.
4. Gently breathe and pay attention to the rise and fall of your in and out breaths. Now instead of the downward facing triangle, imagine your torso as a cylinder, a three-dimensional tube mounted on the upright line of the spine. Mentally explore this and feel

the space between your front and back as you
breathe into it.

5. Now imagine your playing position at your
instrument. Pick it up if you can, or move
to the keyboard or drum kit. Use this new
awareness to explore the three dimensions of
your body as you begin to play. Have you ever
noticed your back, felt your feet on the floor, or
noticed your breathing when playing?

Musicians, writers, and other professionals who work
mostly with their minds have a tendency to lose this sense
of the body as a whole. Guitarists and pianists are particularly prone to this. When your full attention is concentrated
out in front of you, it's easy for the mental map to contract
to a pair of disembodied hands. Bringing the attention back
to encompass the entire body makes playing a completely
different experience.

THE ALEXANDER TECHNIQUE

The Alexander Technique is a method of retraining habitual
patterns of movement and posture, created by Australian
actor F.M. Alexander in the 1890s. The basic concept behind
it is that the human body is a self-supporting mechanism,
like a geodesic dome. Over the course of our lives, the body
is pulled off-balance by patterns of muscular tension that
form and set into habits. By identifying and retraining

these patterns of tension, the body begins to move and balance more freely.

In the early days of the 20th century, eminent figures like the philosopher John Dewey, playwright George Bernard Shaw, and writer Aldous Huxley studied with Alexander and wrote positively of the experience. Actors, musicians, and dancers now study the technique to improve their awareness and control of the body in space, and to develop a more finely tuned mental map.

I started studying Alexander Technique in college, prompted by general curiosity and some concern about my posture. I found a listing in a free magazine at a shop selling crystals, essential oils, and books on meditation. There's actually nothing "New Age" about the Alexander Technique. In fact, it's a very grounded and concrete discipline. But then again, yoga was once viewed by many as a hippy-dippy fringe interest as well, and is now widely accepted for its physical rather than its esoteric benefits.

LEARNING TO WALK, AGAIN

My Alexander teacher Chloe kept a studio in a fourth-floor walkup on West 4th Street in Greenwich Village. She was the calmest person I had ever met, and her quiet apartment was a striking contrast to the gritty street outside: sparsely furnished with white walls, a hardwood floor, and a massage table. She was fortyish and lithe and moved with catlike grace in her bare feet, speaking with just a hint of a genteel

South Carolina accent. The first sessions seemed to be like physical therapy, as I lay on the table and Chloe guided me through a series of stretches and exercises. But there was a striking difference. These exercises weren't about *working* muscles, they were for teaching muscles *not* to work: to allow the body to relax and expand.

When I got up off the table, I felt about a foot taller. It was as if my body had spread out, and I was suddenly aware of myself in three dimensions: feeling my feet on the floor, my head atop my spine, and the space inside my chest, instead of being aware only of what was in front of me. When I left, carrying diagrams of the skeleton marked with arrows and instructions in colored marker, I walked to the subway with the lightest stride I had ever felt in my life.

I worked with Chloe on and off for almost seven years. Over that time she became a friend and mentor, teaching me about much more than how to align my posture. She also taught me to notice and manage my body's reaction to physical and mental stress.

As our work progressed, she became less and less hands-on and would simply direct me verbally. The work became an exploration of mind over matter, realigning and repositioning the body, using thoughts rather than manual adjustment. I was frequently instructed to "ask" a muscle to release: to find it in my mental map and visualize open space there instead of effort. I began to notice how much compressed tension and energy I carried around with me, and to learn ways to release it.

This mental work was a perfect counterpoint to the way I had been learning to practice. Highly focused work on the guitar—or any instrument you touch—concentrates mental energy in the hands. But by expanding that awareness to include the rest of the body, the instrument was incorporated into my mental map and became a natural extension rather than a foreign object.

USING THE BODY NATURALLY

Developing whole-body awareness when you play impacts more than just your posture: it helps you identify and release ingrained patterns of muscle tension and "holding." Tension limits your ability to move freely, affecting everything from the dexterity of your fingers to the flexibility of your upper body, your balance on your feet, and your ability to breathe easily. But these patterns can be so deeply ingrained that we don't notice them at all. Worse yet, they can easily create a vicious cycle. Tension makes it harder to play well, creating frustration, which leads to more tension. However you don't need to study Alexander Technique or yoga to begin to address some of these issues (although I would *definitely* encourage you to explore both).

Like our visualization exercise, it starts with paying attention. How aware are you of your playing posture and physical habits? Have you ever practiced in front of a mirror, or watched yourself on video? If you haven't, do both. It's enlightening, even surprising, and more than a little scary. When you start to observe yourself from this perspective, you will become aware of things you never noticed before.

Chronic tension is probably the worst culprit, and you might be surprised at where you hold it. It took me years to realize that some of my "guitar faces" (you know what I mean, you've seen them!) were coming from tension in my face, not from being deeply into the music. I sang out of the side of my mouth for years, never fully opening my jaw, until I started to learn what "relaxed" felt like. You may never have even thought about the muscles of your face. I certainly hadn't. I see students clenching their jaw and holding their breath as they struggle to execute something, not realizing that part of the reason they struggle is that they're clenching their jaw and holding their breath.

The human body is an amazing mechanism, and it really is just that: a mechanical construct, designed to move in a particular way. If there is an "ideal" technique on any instrument, it's the approach that uses the body the most naturally. I'm always reluctant to use terms like "right" and "wrong" to describe technique. When it comes to guitar, there are idiosyncratic players with amazing skills who play in ways no teacher would ever think to teach.

So technique is not an absolute, but the construction of the human body is. Some ways of moving are more efficient than others, and moving efficiently leads to more fluid and natural playing. From a mechanical perspective, this ergonomic approach makes a lot of sense when you're trying to resolve a technical question.

You don't even need a teacher to explore this. Many students, especially beginners, fall into another trap: thinking that not knowing the "right" way to do something means you can't form an opinion. I've seen so many students struggle with obviously awkward technique in an effort to follow some instruction or other they were given. They know it feels awkward, but assume the problem is their lack of skill, when in fact the problem might be the approach in the first place.

I have yet to have a student tell me that their old way of playing felt better after they've made this kind of adjustment. The new position might not feel natural at first, but there's a difference between unnatural and simply unfamiliar. Being completely relaxed can feel very strange if you're accustomed to feeling tension and don't realize it. Many people find that they've been mistaking stiffness and tension for control. Once they start to let go, they can really feel the difference.

MUSCLE MEMORY

Playing an instrument is like driving a car. With time and repetition, the movements become automatic, triggered by the thought. Moving my fingers to a D chord is as natural as putting my foot on the brake when approaching a red light: the muscles respond to the intended action, not to a specific command to move. Once you've absorbed the basic vocabulary, many of your movements are driven by this "muscle memory."

This is a necessary step in learning to play, but it also creates another challenge: if you try to fight it, muscle memory usually wins.

Muscle memory creates a specific series of muscular movements triggered by an intention. The thought itself sets off a chain of neural impulses through the nervous system, like a signal through a wire. This moves at the speed of electricity, instantaneously as far as we can perceive it. So if you're trying to approach a movement differently, the muscles will respond in the way they've been trained. There's no way to get out ahead of it—unless you break the movement down so far that your muscle memory doesn't engage.

This is the biomechanical reason for slow practice. Rather than changing the neural pathway that directs the muscle movement, we need to establish a new one.

Studies have suggested that we learn motor skills in two stages, fast and slow. "Fast learning" is the immediate improvement we can see over a series of repetitions within a single session. "Slow learning" is the cumulative effect of these fast-learning sessions over time—but this process actually takes place *between* practice sessions, though a mental process called *consolidation*. The physical patterns in muscle memory have already consolidated and have become hardwired.

To create a new pathway, we need to re-engage the fast-learning process and trigger new consolidation. This takes time, and unfortunately when you play at full speed during this transitional period, you are likely to revert to habit. But thanks to the magic of neuroplasticity and the brain's amazing capacity for retraining, the new approach will gain strength. Over time, the new patterns will become more natural until they become as automatic as the old.

Ultimately, ergonomic approaches should always win out because they align better with the body's natural way of moving. When an action is accomplished with less effort, it should be more comfortable than when it required more muscular work. But you need to be tuned into your body enough to feel the difference. So the entire process begins with paying attention.

I frequently ask students what they feel when they play, and most had never thought to ask themselves this question. Rather than giving specific instructions, I will often ask them to just let the body do what it seems to want to do: in other words, to notice any resistance and simply give in to it. There are times when a player can't accomplish something because of a lack of control or coordination, but that's a very different feeling than the sense that your muscles would rather be moving in another way. Slowing down enough to really notice what's happening allows you to differentiate between automatic and intentional movements, and to practice in a deliberately repetitive way to set up the fast-learning/slow-learning process.

TRAPS

As you begin to observe your technique more specifically,

the first thing you will start to notice is how often you're tuned out! Keep in mind that your goal in the beginning isn't to change anything, just to notice what's happening. There are a number of things you might discover, but here are three of the most common specific traps.

1. **Holding your breath**
   This is the big one. Unless you're singing or playing a wind instrument, your breathing can be completely disconnected from your playing. It shouldn't be; in fact, your ability to play musically has everything to do with your breath. The whole body tenses when you hold your breath, making it harder to play with fluidity. The tension also makes it harder to breathe freely, compounding the problem into a vicious cycle.

   Thankfully, breathing is a great way to get muscles to relax. Try to imagine breathing into your lower torso, lower back, or shoulders. This isn't really a question of anatomy but of visualization, using the breath as a tool. Remember that what we're really working on is your perception, and your ability to create a sense of relaxed openness anywhere in the body. Breath is a powerful way to work with both.

2. **Not moving the body**
   This is related to the breath as well. One of the

biggest traps we can fall into as musicians is to disconnect from our bodies *and* to disconnect parts of the body from each other. Playing well uses the entire body, not just the muscles we use to play the instrument but also the muscles that support them. We need to be balanced on our feet or our seat in a way that allows the upper body to stay open enough for the hands to move freely. All of this is connected to our breathing.

Aside from the mechanical aspect, there's also a musical one. No matter what instrument or style of music you play, you want to have a strong sense of rhythm. This comes from internalizing the beat, feeling the pulse in your body. Rhythm is the most concrete and physical aspect of music, and while it's something we can count and measure, it's not only mathematical. We've established that rhythm comes naturally to human beings, whether you think you "have it" or not. We breathe and walk in rhythm. Our hearts beat in time, and there's a cadence and groove to speech. So you already have rhythm in your body, and when you relax into it, you can start to move with it naturally. (Refer back to Chapter 3, "On Practicing," for a more specific discussion of rhythm.)

3. **Locking the neck and shoulders**

   This is another common problem, especially for percussive, hand-intensive instruments like guitar and piano. We've already discussed how focusing on the hands can make you lose your sense of the rest of the body. It's also easy to "brace" the muscles of the neck and shoulders in an unconscious effort to support the effort coming from the hands.

   This is counterproductive, of course, because you'd actually have more support from the shoulder muscles if they were relaxed and able to move freely. Over the long term, the muscles of the forearm can engage to compensate for the lack of support from the shoulders. The entire system from hands up to shoulders begins to break down. Small muscles are supposed to lead and be supported by larger muscle groups to keep them from working too hard. When those small muscles lose that support, they begin to overcompensate. Over time this can lead to chronic pain or larger repetitive strain problems like tendinitis and carpal tunnel syndrome. (I detail my own experience with repetitive strain in Chapter 7, "Purist and Maverick".)

You may have other issues of your own, but regardless of the problem, the first step in solving it is to pay attention. Keep an open mind in all your explorations, and remember that the body does have a mechanical logic and a natural way of moving. If a teacher suggests that you play in a way that feels deeply unnatural, pay attention to what you're feeling. There may be an adjustment you need to make. Trust the inherent wisdom of your body, cultivate your mental map, and be clear on the difference between uncomfortable and unfamiliar. You'll be a better and healthier musician for it.

CHAPTER 5

THE BIG PICTURE

HEAR THE MUSIC, NOT JUST THE NOTES

My technical abilities as a player haven't really changed since my early 20s. My first 10 years with the guitar were intense and concentrated, a constant effort to expand the boundaries of what I was capable of. This gave me the playing ability I needed to be a professional musician, and for that goal it was essential.

But some of the most important skills musicians develop are mental rather than technical, and aren't dependent on your ability. Instead, these skills allow you to make the most of what you're able to do. And while "chops" develop up to a certain point, skill as a musician can keep growing for a lifetime.

The difference between how I play now and the way I played 20 years ago is in my perception of music and my ability to react to it. In the very beginning, the mechanics of where to put my fingers and how to sound the notes were all I could think about. Playing with a group for the first time, I found it nerve-wracking to try to pay attention to my own part against everything else that was going on! But over time, I learned to listen to the other instruments while simultaneously keeping track of my part. The physical part of playing started to require less effort as my ear grew more able to process multiple things at once.

This expanding perspective began to include not just the parts themselves, but also how they worked together to form a coherent whole. It included the ability to take a larger view, along with an understanding of the individual elements: the perspective of the general commanding the battle as well as of the infantryman on the front lines, the orchestra conductor as well as the second violinist. This perspective comes with time and experience, and the only qualification to develop it is—you guessed it—a willingness to listen.

"MOMENTS WHEN YOU COULD ALMOST RELAX"

I wanted to know about everything when I was learning to play. I read books and magazines cover to cover, and listened to all the music, even if I didn't always understand it. I still had my favorite sounds, the things that moved me emotionally, but I wanted to be open to everything. I discovered jazz and ambient music, and my own experiments in improvisation had started to reveal all kinds of new musical possibilities.

(For more on this subject, see Chapter 6, "The Conversation.")

I admired the creativity of people who seemed to be inventing their own sonic worlds. Going to college in 1980s New York gave me access to a thriving avant-garde "downtown" scene at places like the Knitting Factory and the Kitchen, as well as venerable jazz clubs like the Blue Note and the Village Vanguard. But much of what I heard there was over my head. I couldn't follow what was going on, but I knew there had to be something I couldn't hear that would somehow tie it all together.

One of the most striking shows I ever saw was a performance in 1989 by pianist Cecil Taylor and his band at the Knitting Factory, at the time a downstairs jazz dive on Houston Street in lower Manhattan. Taylor was an avant-garde hero and a controversial figure in the jazz world, trained in classical composition but schooled in the clubs. He is considered one of the few musicians to successfully fuse jazz improvisation with thorny, dissonant European "art music" modernism. Had I known this walking in, I might have had a better idea of what to expect.

Onstage, the familiar jazz band instrumentation of piano, horns, string bass, and drums was set up. But when they started to play, the sound was like nothing I had ever heard. I wasn't sure I liked it—in fact, I wasn't even sure what to think of it. It was chaotic and wild, and seemed not to have any organizing elements at all. The next day I looked up the show in the events listings of the *New*

Yorker magazine. I was struck by the description of Taylor's music: a sound like a large shape-shifting object, heavy and ponderous and sometimes threatening, with "moments that were almost unbearable and moments when you could almost relax."

That memorable description captured my experience of the performance perfectly. The music was hard to listen to and vaguely uncomfortable, and I can't say I wasn't glad when it was over. But as inscrutable as it was, it was clear to me that the musicians onstage understood what was happening in a way that I didn't. They could hear a larger context that made sense of the chaos.

LONG, STRANGE TRIPS

I was introduced to the music and culture of the Grateful Dead during my first year of college. While I knew about hippies in tie-dye, I knew very little about the band's experimental streak. The Dead's treatment of songs as outlines for improvisation alongside fully composed parts actually put them closer to a jazz group than a rock band, in philosophy if not in sound.

Many songs included long instrumental sections that might be radically different each time they were played. These were often not "solos" in the usual sense, although Jerry Garcia's mercurial lead guitar lines generally led the way. These were open vehicles: a basic framework that started with elements of the song, then progressed through a series of metamorphoses before finally returning to the composed theme.

It might be easy to dismiss these parts as meandering and aimless, but that misses the point. There may not have been an overarching structure—in fact, the whole idea was to leave the structure behind—but there was constant interaction between the instruments. The music was held together by the fact that each player's note choices were being directed by the choices of the others.

There were composed parts and themes to the songs, but they would still be approached differently from one performance to another. This is ultimately a jazz dynamic: the musicians follow a map, but not a detailed one, in which there are multiple paths through the same territory and all landmarks are subject to change or reinvention.

FINDING THE PATH

Musical relationships can be seen as layers, in which a broader framework is fleshed out by specific melodic, rhythmic, and chordal patterns. When musicians improvise, they explore alternate routes through the same territory, relying on the map and the breadcrumbs provided by the other players. This is what I was hearing in the music of Cecil Taylor and the Grateful Dead: musicians exploring the musical terrain, following the contours of the landscape. This is a very useful way to think about music, even when playing songs with composed parts.

Composition and songwriting start with the same exploratory process, but then decide on a consistent route and build a clearly marked path. Writing and improvising are both enhanced by the ability to see the larger "shape" of the song, as well as the possibilities implied by the interaction of the individual parts. Chord progressions suggest melodic options. An unaccompanied melody implies harmony and suggests a rhythmic background. All of these details need to fit into a larger context to create a complete piece of music.

In fact, we could say that every piece of music is a web of interdependent and layered relationships: melody to chords, chords to melody, both to rhythm, and all to *form*, the overarching structure. Whether the process of learning to hear and understand these relationships is conscious or intuitive, the ability to do so requires understanding two crucial concepts:

1. Every musical gesture is related to the other musical elements that accompany or follow it.
2. All the musical elements have a *function* within the complete whole, determined by the relationships between them.

Let's explore this in greater depth with a discussion of musical *function*.

FUNCTION, MOVEMENT, AND EXPECTATION

"Function" has to do with the way music moves. A particular chord or note might potentially go to any other chord or note, but in most cases goes to one of a limited number of options.

Certain patterns tend to progress in a particular way, in that each change determines a range of usual possibilities for the next change. So function refers to the way that each note or chord sets up the others within the unfolding progression. When we hear something unusual or unexpected, the music plays on the listener's expectation of a more predictable outcome and opts for another.

In the late 19th century, the Austrian musician and theorist Heinrich Schenker proposed that tonal music could be organized into a hierarchy. He suggested that a large-scale form like a sonata or a symphony could be broken down to primary "structural" notes, with secondary notes filling in the specific details. According to his theory, all *tonal* music has the same movement, from a point of rest to a point of tension and finally resolution. He found this movement at every level: within the notes of a melody, in the progression of a chord sequence, and in the sections of a longer piece of music.

This doesn't mean the notes that aren't "structural" don't matter—the specific notes are, of course, the details that differentiate one piece of music from another. But the larger gestures and structure explain why the music unfolds the way it does.

You don't actually need a deep knowledge of music theory to understand these concepts. You can start by listening for the cycles and patterns that define sections of a song. This should give you a sense of the harmonic "home." This will be a *key center* that creates a sense of resolution when the music arrives there. Once you've established that, you can start to hear how the unfolding sequence of melodic gestures and accompanying chords create a sense of movement around that center. In the context of a whole song, you'll find the same kind of musical layers Schenker did, working outward from the most specific details of the melody to the larger patterns that define the overall "form."

Even when the music isn't built on the movement of chords, this idea of a large-scale structure—with an unfolding of tension and release through foreground and background details—can still apply. Many modern pop songs use a repeating cycle of just three or four chords, sometimes for the entire song. This doesn't provide the same sense of *harmonic* (chordal) movement on a larger scale. Instead, the arrangements will often use layers of repetitive rhythmic "loops" that propel the music forward by changing the sonic texture instead of the harmony.

TEXTURE

A great deal of modern pop and electronic music uses these repetitive cycles and layered rhythms to shape the unfolding of the big picture. In such cases, musical *texture* is used to enhance or even take the place of harmonic progression.

Formally trained musicians might use the term "texture" to describe the way different elements of the music work together. For example, a melody against a simple accompaniment creates one type of texture, "homophonic."

Multiple melodies in conversation create a "polyphonic" texture. This definition also introduces the idea of musical foreground and background—melody and accompaniment, and the way this line can be blurred as the parts interact.

But for our purposes, let's think of texture in terms of two broad aspects: density and *color*. "Density" describes the level of activity in the music. A small number of instruments playing just a few notes might produce an open, spacious sound. More notes from the same instruments, or more instruments, might make the sound busier. More rhythmic activity could have the same effect. Imagine a saxophone playing rapid flurries of notes, or a drummer playing a virtuosic solo. On the other hand, an orchestra of a hundred musicians can conjure up the stillness of outer space with a single soft chord. The "moments when you could almost relax" in the music of Cecil Taylor were placid sections where the texture thinned out and the chaos abated before building once again to a cacophonous climax.

"Color" is a tricky term to use when applied to music. Some people really do experience a synesthetic sense of actual colors when they listen to music, but I'm using the word more generally to draw a parallel. It can be as difficult to describe the difference in sound between a flute and a clarinet as it might be to describe the difference between red and blue. Some musicians might use the word "tone" and others might refer to "tone color." Your perception of the differences is more important than the exact language you use, but the point is that these contrasts can be used to create movement or articulate form just as harmony and rhythm can.

WHAT DOES THIS MEAN TO YOU?

Learning music is a lot like learning a new language. Our ability to be understood is determined by our vocabulary, and our understanding of grammatical context. At first we learn the meaning of individual words. This is like learning the notes. Over time we learn to form sentences, and then how to express and develop ideas.

Being aware of the structure of the music reinforces a performer's ability to convey the emotion of the song, by expressing the inherent dynamics and ebb and flow of energy. This is one of the things that naturally intuitive musicians do without thinking about it. The ability to "just feel it" might be the strongest natural ability of the musically gifted. Musical aptitude is a lot like mechanical aptitude, an ability to see relationships in the same way that allows some people to look at a pile of wood and see a house.

Do you struggle with learning songs because you can't remember the chord sequences? Do you find your improvisations meandering and unfocused? Do your songs seem like they don't hang together? In any of these cases, it's possible that you're missing the larger perspective that will tie all the pieces together.

Even if you don't face any of these particular challenges, it's worth asking yourself how much you can really hear in a piece of music. Are you aware of foreground and background details? Can you break down a melody into its component phrases and sub-phrases, or organize all the sections of a song to articulate a clear form? These are all skills that will make you a better and more tuned-in musician, no matter how simple or complex the music you play might be.

CHAPTER 6

THE CONVERSATION

LEARNING TO IMPROVISE

When I was first learning to play, I had a vague concept of what "improvisation" meant. The songs I loved had exciting guitar solos, but I knew them as compositions and learned to play them note-for-note. Many of the players I admired would do the same onstage, knowing that their fans—like me—wanted to hear these solos as they had been recorded. Pink Floyd's David Gilmour played sinuous melodies I can still sing from memory, and the middle solo break of "Comfortably Numb" still gives me chills. Rush's Alex Lifeson was absolutely faithful to his recordings, and I have a vivid memory of jumping out of my seat with excitement at the first notes of "Limelight" when I saw Rush play in 1983. I learned every nuance of Jimmy Page's epic solo on Led Zeppelin's "Stairway To Heaven," and was somewhat disappointed by the difference in the version on the live album *The Song Remains The Same*. (In fact, it hadn't.)

What I didn't fully understand then was that, even though those parts were as fluid and sounded as composed as the rest of the music, many of them had been completely or mostly improvised. My favorite players weren't painstakingly choosing each note. They were opening themselves up to spontaneous creation, and the universe obliged.

Improvisation is arguably the purest form of musical expression: a direct connection between ideas and sounds in the moment, with no goal other than to maintain the flow. I do my best playing when I'm improvising—or rather, I should say that my best moments as a player happen during improvisation. Despite all my training as a classical musician playing notes off a page, some of my most formative musical experiences had to do with making it up as I went along.

THE NOISE QUARTET

I had a musical epiphany when I was 16. My parents had agreed to send me to a summer program at the Berklee College of Music in Boston, a six-week immersion course. It was my first experience with serious study outside of my guitar lessons. It was also my first time away from home on my own, and could have been an opportunity for me to get into lots of trouble. The school was in a pretty rough neighborhood in those days, and I found the grittiness and sense of danger more than a little thrilling. I got myself mugged one night by some rough friends of a girl I thought I was meeting for a date. But thankfully, I was serious about music. I wasn't a very diligent student outside my guitar lessons, and probably skipped as many classes as I attended. But the greatest lesson I learned that summer occurred not in a classroom but in a rehearsal room, jamming with my friends.

Across the hall from me were three guys sharing a triple room. Tom was a bass player and looked like a blond Geddy Lee, the virtuoso bassist of my favorite band Rush. Mark was a gangly drummer, a jokester with tremendous energy and serious chops as a player. Andrew played both bass and guitar, and he was into music I had never heard before. He introduced me to Frank Zappa's extended guitar improvisations, King Crimson's intellectual but accessible polyrhythmic grooves, and the psychedelic soundscapes of early Pink Floyd.

Our first attempts at jamming were lots of fun. We tried our best to play songs we knew in common, which for long-haired kids in 1984 was Led Zeppelin, Van Halen, Black Sabbath, and Rush. It was definitely a thrill to tackle something as challenging as Rush's "2112 Overture," and learning to navigate the complex timing as a group was an education for all of us. We had a good time, but it was clear we were reaching for something we weren't quite ready to master.

The solution that changed everything may have been Andrew's idea. Much of what we were playing was power trio music, which didn't have a second guitar, so it might have been a way to find a space for himself. He was also the one who was most familiar with exploratory, improvisational music.

We were all learning about jazz that summer. Berklee had started as a jazz school, and while it was in transition in the 1980s, the program was still jazz-oriented. In one session, someone suggested we try having a musical "conversation" rather than playing a song we knew.

This is, of course, the essence of jazz. Ultimately a jazz song is a framework, a suggested topic for discussion. There is generally a "head" melody and specific chords that go with it, but everything is open to improvisation and no two performances are the same. There may be one soloist at a time, but every player is reacting to every other. What you hear dictates what you play, as in a conversation.

It would start with the drums, Mark setting up a beat. Tom would join in on bass, the two of them working together. Bass gives pitch to the rhythm, while drums give the bass punch. Andrew and I would play over this—sometimes with both of us on guitar, sometimes with him playing bass through a Rat distortion pedal. And I explored.

We recorded these sessions and afterwards we'd listen back in their room. I would hear something on the tape that caught my ear and think: *I played that?* Over time, we actually started to sound like a band. There were themes, and grooves, and goofy songs like "Sick Moose," which began with a *glissando* (slide) from Andrew's distorted bass faded in with the volume knob as the rest of us chanted. It was noisy, adolescent, and glorious.

We called ourselves the Noise Quartet and developed our own language of inside jokes and catchphrases, as all young men do. But most of all, we grew as musicians. I wish I still had those recordings. It may have started off as four kids goofing around, but we were learning to apply core principles of improvisation that have stayed with me ever since.

MUSIC FOR PEOPLE

In 1988, I was a performance major in classical guitar at the Aaron Copland School of Music in Queens, NY. While I was committed to my classical studies, I had continued to develop an interest in improvised music. New York had a thriving avant-garde jazz scene in the 1980s and I would go to see experimental musicians like pianist Cecil Taylor, saxophonist John Zorn, and guitarist Bill Frisell at the original Knitting Factory jazz club on Houston Street in lower Manhattan. (See Chapter 5, "The Big Picture," for more on the impact this had on me.)

My guitar teacher at the time, Ben Verdery, was (and still is) a very open-minded musician, as interested in pushing boundaries as he was in interpreting Bach. I was still deeply into the music and approach of "jam bands" like the Grateful Dead and the Allman Brothers. So I was surrounded by explorers, and I wanted to take my own explorations further. When I heard that the jazz cellist David Darling was teaching an improvisation workshop at a small college in central Pennsylvania, I jumped at the chance to meet and learn from another musical adventurer.

In the late 1960s, David Darling had played with the Paul Winter Consort, an extremely innovative ensemble for its time and often considered the first "New Age" jazz group. The Consort took a familiar configuration of a jazz quartet—saxophone, guitar, bass, and percussion, in this case—and added classical and "world music" instruments like cello, oboe, classical guitar, and Indian percussion. Darling went on to record numerous projects with German jazz label ECM, among others, and founded Music for People in 1986 with the aim of introducing musicians and non-musicians alike to improvisation.

The daylong Music for People workshop I attended that fall drew a diverse group of professional musicians, amateurs, and people with no musical experience at all. I had never been to a class that included people with such a wide range of knowledge and ability. That was the first lesson in itself: what we were going to learn had very little to do with whether or not you could play.

Skilled players might know how to make sounds, but not necessarily how to decide which sounds to make. So the ability to play the instrument well and the ability to improvise freely are two different things! Darling's great insight was that people find improvisation intimidating because they are afraid of making a mistake. Unskilled players share the same inhibition, but if you give them an easy way to make sounds, the playing field is effectively leveled. So the group was presented with a set of percussion instruments:

bells, drums, gongs, xylophones, Bundt pans—anything that might make an interesting sound when struck, but didn't require training or skill.

It was time to make music.

"ONE QUALITY SOUND"

Any improvisation is ultimately just a series of sounds. Of course, there's a lot more involved when there's a particular musical setting to fit into, but at the core, it really is that simple. Putting notes together isn't all that different from putting words together into phrases and sentences. We learn to speak by imitating the speech we hear and the things we read.

Playing music is ultimately the same thing. Just as we "speak" by stringing together a basic vocabulary, using letters to form words and words to form sentences, we use notes to form *phrases* and phrases to form *melodies*. The process is equally intuitive in either case, even if we don't realize it. The difference is that we speak before we can read, and we can make sounds with our voices without needing to be taught how. Once you can make a sound and develop a vocabulary, the rest is expression.

One of the core lessons of the Music for People workshop was the idea of "one quality sound." In other words, a player needs only to focus on making one sound at a time.

Taken as a single isolated idea, that's not enough to make a piece of music hang together. There are many musical factors that make a sound "quality," including an understanding of musical context. And just as with speech, we need to be taught to form "words" and to use them to form coherent ideas. But it all begins with the single sound. This is why starting with simple percussion was so effective, because it took away the skill barrier and allowed the players to focus on interacting.

Early elementary music classes often incorporate xylophones or other pitched percussion instruments. They're easy to play and make a pleasing sound. This makes them great for encouraging musical exploration: just hit it and see what happens. You may have seen a child do the same with a piano or a guitar. Kids aren't intimidated by the fact that they don't know "how to play" —not knowing what to do doesn't stop them from doing it. For the adult student, simple percussion instruments are a great way to deal with the "option anxiety" of having too many potential sounds to make.

THE IMPROMPTU QUARTET

For the final part of the workshop, the more skilled players formed small ensembles and were instructed to play together on the spot. Ordinarily, even a jazz group has some agreed-on parameters: a specific melody that can be embellished and a set of chords that at least form a starting point. This music was meant to simply happen, without any discussion beforehand. In some settings, this might lead to chaos, although sometimes that's the desired effect.

In this case, the day's lessons and the collective experience of the musicians all came into play. My group combined my guitar with a collection of winds: flute, clarinet, and saxophone. These instruments might play together in a variety of combinations, but the quartet setting was unusual and it was probably the first time any of us had tried it.

It's striking how musical instincts can kick in under the right circumstances. In the years since that workshop, I've seen similar things happen again and again, even from students with very limited playing experience. We've all heard music around us our entire lives. We've been absorbing the sounds all the while, even if we don't realize it. I've seen it in my own playing, finding that I knew how to play parts I had never consciously learned—even if I wasn't consciously trying to duplicate them. We all have an idea of how notes might work together, even if we have limited experience actually playing them. This isn't a conscious process—we absorb through repeated exposure, just like we learn to speak.

Our little quartet made some amazing music that day. With nothing else to follow but what we were hearing at that moment, everyone simply tuned in and tried to make a sound that complemented the others. Of course, it didn't sound like an organized song. It was more of what composers might call a "tone poem." But my memory is that we created a sound like a multi-faceted crystal suspended in the air between us, slowly turning in the light and reflecting changing colors as it breathed like a living thing.

The exercises in the workshop had led all the participants to a place where we could easily make music together.

By eliminating specific parameters, we were freed of the requirement for agreed-upon patterns—just as my Noise Quartet had done five years before. The music was certainly different, but not the way it was made: make a sound, listen, and then make another. Adopting this approach can fundamentally change your playing the way it did mine.

EXERCISES FOR IMPROVISATION

1. Play something simple: a single sustained note, or a strummed chord. Listen as the sound dies away. Notice the silence that follows before you play again.

2. Repeat the sound, adding rhythm without changing the pitch. No matter what you're playing, treat it like a drum. Your variables are *only* how loudly to play the note, how long it lasts, and how long to wait before playing the next one.

3. Begin to add more sounds. Introduce another drum, another note, or another chord. Start by alternating between two or three sounds. If you're playing a melody instrument, you can choose a segment of a scale or existing melody, but don't just run up and down the scale! Pay attention to the "shape" of the melody you're creating, listening for smaller and larger steps or leaps up and down. Remember to leave

space, allowing each idea to finish and die away before beginning another.

4. If you're able to do this in a group setting, experiment with having your own "conversations." Two or more players might alternate their musical statements, or play together and listen to the interaction. "Quality" now has a lot to do with how naturally your statements work with and against the others.

5. Above all, keep your sense of discovery and play! The Music for People handbook is called "Return to Child" because a childlike approach is the most effective here.

Listen, observe, and explore, but don't judge. The concept of "Beginner's Mind" introduced in Chapter 9 creates a powerful and effective mindset for doing this work.

CHAPTER 7

THE PURIST & THE MAVERICK

STYLE, AUTHENTICITY, & EXPRESSION

Classical guitar is a beautiful and fiendishly demanding discipline. I studied seriously for 10 years, and I did well. I graduated first in my class at the Aaron Copland School at the City University of New York. At the Manhattan School of Music, I won the Rose Augustine award for promising young classical guitarists twice. I had distinguished myself at a top conservatory among serious guitar students from around the world. And I did love it, even when I didn't.

But looking back, I realize that I didn't love it with my heart. I loved the idea of being a classical musician, as stodgy as that sounds to most people. The music absolutely did touch me, and I got a great sense of accomplishment from playing it well. But my relationship with the classical guitar was a marriage of convenience. There was certainly affection there, and I thought I could see a life for myself in it. But in retrospect, I think I also saw it as a way to become sophisticated, worldly, and accomplished. It was the next step in my journey of self-discovery, but it was also the next role that I tried on like a new suit to see how it fit. I might have worn it well, but it ultimately wasn't me.

You may have never questioned why you play the music you play, or how you approach it. Many people are happy just learning songs they love, and that simple enjoyment is reason enough. But the music you play can also be part of who you are, and getting to know how to play like *you* can be the biggest step forward you'll ever take.

YOU CAN'T RASGUEADO LIKE GRINGO

In early 1994, the year after I completed my Masters degree, I was accepted to perform in a master class at Yale University. The "master class" is a tradition in classical music, in which students perform for eminent players for critique in front of an audience. This could be highly intimidating, especially when playing for a maestro with a reputation for exacting standards. But that's the point, and it's well worth the chance to learn from some of the best musicians in the world.

The maestro in this case was an eminent American guitarist, one of the few to attract attention outside of the very closed world of classical guitar. He was a successful concert artist, known both for premiering new music and for his work on film soundtracks—including one with particular resonance for me and many of my guitar-playing peers who were straddling the worlds of classical and rock music.

The class was in the recital hall at the Yale School of Music, and featured several students performing for an audience of about two hundred guitarists and aficionados. I had played the same piece, a flamenco-influenced sonata by the 20th century Spanish composer Joaquin Turina, in another master class and at my graduation recital from the Manhattan School. I knew the music well, and had worked out a careful interpretation.

However, there was one important detail that had escaped me: the use of the Spanish strum, or *rasgueado*. You know the sound: imagine a dramatically strummed Spanish guitar, with the individual fingers of the right hand quickly and repeatedly striking the strings. It's a difficult technique to master, but essential to properly evoke the spirit of flamenco.

What I didn't know was that the maestro had studied under Pepe Romero of the celebrated Romero family, titans of Spanish guitar who had fled the Spanish dictator Franco's totalitarian regime in the 1950s to settle in California. This should have been a great opportunity to get closer to the source, but I was not mentally prepared for the judgment of a purist.

I was never fully comfortable onstage with the classical guitar, and a high-pressure situation only made it worse. My hands were clammy and seemed much further away than usual. I'm sure I wasn't at my best, but it wasn't a disaster. My playing had been acceptable to other masters I had played for, including the internationally renowned founder of the guitar program at the Juilliard School. So reasonably enough, I thought it was OK. Not this time. The maestro chided me on my strumming technique, then looked knowingly at the audience and said: "You can't *rasgueado* like gringo!"

This got the big laugh he had intended, and I wanted to crawl under my chair. I was so distracted by the feeling of humiliation that I didn't retain anything else he said. But there were lessons to take away.

AN UNEXPECTED TURNING POINT

It's worth mentioning again that I had worked on the same piece with two equally eminent experts, who had voiced no objections to my technique. But if the music is meant to evoke flamenco, it's reasonable to suggest that it would be better for the technique to be faithful to the style. I could have explored the context of the piece more thoroughly. If I had done my due diligence, I would have been more aware of what was stylistically appropriate and what wasn't. From the perspective of someone who really knew the style, I hadn't gone deep enough. However, you could also view his perspective as the view of a purist rather than a creative interpreter.

My skin should have been a little thicker. I allowed my ego to get in the way and so I lost the opportunity to really learn something new. I could have chosen to take or leave his input, but I didn't have to take it personally.

Regardless, the experience turned out to be my last as a classical musician. Some weeks later, I started to feel an unprecedented level of pain in my hands. Occasional strain was one thing, but this was something else. The pain spread up my arms and into my shoulders and back. The diagnosis was a repetitive strain injury: acute thoracic outlet syndrome, a compression of the nerves between the collarbone and first rib. I quit playing to endure six frustrating months of physical therapy and introspection.

When I was able to play again, I had to make a choice between the two paths I had explored: not just the difference between the classical and the electric guitar, but the difference between two competing musical universes. In one, the performance felt like a standard to be met. In the other, it was pure expression, an exploration of the unknown. This is an oversimplification, but viewed in that light, it wasn't a difficult choice.

THE PHILOSOPHICAL SPLIT

There's a fundamental difference in values between kinds of musicians, one that mirrors the philosophical divisions in our society as a whole. One side favors order, structure, and excellence in execution. The other favors free expression, individuality, and an embrace of the unfamiliar. One places the greatest value on the end result, while the other is more focused on the process of creation.

This might be simplistically viewed as the difference between the classical approach, where the music is written out, and the popular one, in which it isn't. You could think of it as the difference between schooled and self-taught musicians, or between the conservatory and the night-club. But it's not that clear cut, and the divisions don't fall along stylistic lines in the way you might think. There are blues players who absolutely insist on a certain sound and approach to be faithful to an established model, and "clas-sical" musicians who push the boundaries of what music can sound like and still be called music. Some players in every genre want every detail worked out, leaving nothing to chance. Others find the greatest power in spontaneity and the inspiration of the moment.

I learned lessons from my classical education that have shaped my playing and musical philosophy ever since. I learned discipline, structure, and subtlety from playing classical guitar. I learned to shape my sound with nothing but my mind and hands, with no effects or gear to lean on. I learned how much more there was to playing music than just the notes. But I am an improviser at heart, and still feel that I play my best when I'm flowing rather than thinking. To reach that level of flow, the technique has to be solidly enough in place that you can forget it.

Classical discipline teaches you to learn every detail of the music, and playing the right notes according to the instructions of the score is only the beginning. There are decisions to be made in the expression of every note, and the difference between a rote performance and a memorable one is in how convincing those decisions are to an audience. Virtuosity is a requirement in classical music; it's a given that the player can execute the notes. But the player's choices are what make a performance sing, by communicating individuality and emotion. When the music becomes as familiar as a story you've known by heart since childhood, you're free to focus on the art in the delivery. You can be mindful of the process rather than the execution.

There's a school of thought that believes every player needs to be well acquainted with the work of important musicians of the past. There's something to be said for that perspective: no music exists without roots, and a deep knowledge of musical history can really expand a player's vocabulary. But in some ways, this is a purist's view. For example, jazz music has evolved from its roots in the streets of New Orleans to branches all over the musical world, and what exactly constitutes "jazz" is a topic for an entirely different book. But improvisation is a common thread through all its permutations, and the essence of improvisation is to create something that didn't exist before. Most of the revered figures in jazz—really, in any genre—were innovators, mavericks who created something new and different.

At the same time, even the most unique musicians have learned from the masters who came before them. So the challenge for every creative player is to strike a balance between your own individual standard and a bar that's been set by others.

SKILL AND STYLE

Does it really matter whether you approach a style faithfully? Is it possible to play "well" without a versatile technique and knowledge of musical history and context? Do you need to know flamenco to play a Spanish classical piece? Do you need to know Delta blues to play a rock groove? Do you need to understand bebop to play contemporary jazz? These are worthwhile questions to ask, and the answers have everything to do with perspective and context.

The question to ask first is: what are you aiming for? Are you exploring your own voice and your own expression, or are you trying to learn from (and measure up to) a standard of excellence and a tradition?

The two aren't mutually exclusive. Excellence in technique can be seen as a vehicle for the expression of personal style. And a performer can have an individual style and still be held to an objective standard. Olympic gymnasts are all scored by the same criteria, but the best certainly show their own personality as they execute their routines. The same could be said of classical musicians at the highest level. Every genre of music has its canon, a standard repertoire that provides a model to be absorbed and understood. So perhaps there isn't such a divide after all, but a predisposition, a tendency to lean to one side or the other.

In popular music, the musicians who have the most impact are often the ones that break the mold. They don't live up to a standard; they set a new one. It might have nothing to do with skill: the punk revolution of the late 1970s and the explosive success of Nirvana in the 1990s proved that virtuosity is not a requirement. On the other hand, 1960s icon Jimi Hendrix, ground-breaking jazz bassist Jaco Pastorius, and hard-rock innovator Eddie Van Halen all had spectacular abilities on their instruments. What made them iconic was the same thing that made Elvis a legend. Chops can dazzle, but force of personality and a compelling sound can change the landscape.

BECOMING YOURSELF

If you don't consider yourself a "serious" musician, or don't have career aspirations in music, you may not have ever considered these things. Most people choose something they want to play and imitate it. Their ultimate goal is to reproduce the original as faithfully as possible, and it's very satisfying to be able to do it. Perfect execution can be its own reward.

But the pursuit of perfection can also be a trap. It's easy to minimize your own accomplishments because of the bar you're measuring yourself against. High standards lead to high levels of skill and are important to your development as a player. But it's also important to balance your standards and your motivation. If you find yourself getting discouraged instead of inspired, you might be focusing on the wrong things.

When push came to shove, for me it wasn't as satisfying to execute a perfect rasgueado as it was to create. I wanted to improvise a great solo, or write a good song. But both of those things require skill in execution and knowledge of the great accomplishments of others. I did ultimately decide that to be satisfied as a musician and artist, I wanted to create my own standard rather than be measured against someone else's. But this was after I had invested years in developing enough technique to be able to explore freely.

This was the biggest lesson of all: that the purist and the maverick both have valid views. You may be predisposed toward one or the other, but you don't have to choose a side. Ultimately, the best way to become a creatively fulfilled musician is to learn from the past, but create your own future.

CHAPTER 8

SIMPLICITY & AUTHORITY

THE "EASY" THINGS AREN'T ALWAYS

Sometimes the moments that put you in your place are so subtle and friendly that you don't realize how thoroughly you've been trounced.

When I was playing and studying the complex music that I did in my early 20s, I thought of myself as an advanced and sophisticated musician. But I was taught a powerful and humbling lesson on simplicity by a group of folk musicians in the sandy pines near Plymouth, Massachusetts. That lesson was driven home even more powerfully by the contrast with my experience at a jazz workshop the week before.

STANDARDS AND JAMMING

By the summer of 1989 I was deep into my classical guitar studies, but I had continued to develop an ongoing interest in jazz and composition. When I heard that jazz guitar giant Pat Martino would be teaching a week-long seminar at the National Guitar Summer Workshop in Connecticut, I registered right away. Seen by many as a genius, Martino had suffered a brain aneurysm in 1980 that left him with amnesia and took away his ability to play. The experience of reconstructing his musical skills had given him a unique perspective that I wanted to learn from. His chosen idiom was bebop, a highly complex and virtuosic style of jazz, but his musical ideas seemed to transcend genre. I was hungry for creative stimulation and excited to explore rarified musical territory.

Unfortunately, Martino's health was not good that summer and he was unable to teach the workshop. He was replaced by Mick Goodrick, a brilliant guitarist who headed up the guitar program at the Berklee College of Music in Boston. I have to admit I don't remember much from the classes, and I imagine much of the material was over my head at the time. I was interested enough to want to be there, but I suspect I didn't have the background knowledge I needed to really make the most of the information.

I certainly didn't fit in with the hardcore jazzers, all playing similar semi-hollowbody electric guitars and carrying copies of *The Real Book*, a jazz bible containing lead sheets to hundreds of standard tunes. A "standard" is a song that has become part of the repertoire that every competent player is expected to know. Jazz students learn many of these standards inside and out in multiple keys as they get to know the vocabulary. I had a passing familiarity with a handful of the tunes from my own summer at Berklee and my high school jazz band. But since I had been majoring in classical guitar, it wasn't an area I had focused on. While I appreciated bebop—or at least, tried to—I didn't speak the language with any fluency.

I tried jamming with other players with varying degrees of success. While most of them were far more familiar with the style, it was striking to me that many of them didn't play together very well. There seemed to be very little spontaneous playing. Everyone seemed to need the book, and they talked about how they learned this or that "lick" from different players. When I tried to lead one open-ended jam, one of the guys told me there hadn't been enough chords to play over to keep him interested. However, it seemed to me that without a chord sequence to tell him which patterns to plug in, this particular player didn't have much to say.

In fairness, I was also coming from a foundation in improvisational rock, where extended jamming without a specific chord sequence is more a norm. (Many rock musicians wouldn't be able to keep up with all the chords in the average jazz standard.) Jazz musicians learn to "play the changes," meaning they can follow a series of chords and adjust their note choices accordingly. But jazz is also full of open "vamps," in which the music stays on one or two chords. Jazz musicians as revered as trumpeter and bandleader Miles Davis had experimented with open structures on a single, unchanging *tonal center*. The sense of movement in the music comes from rhythm and melody, often in dynamic waves, that build to a crashing peak and then subside, over and over. (See my description of a Cecil Taylor performance in Chapter 5, "The Big Picture.")

The open-ended improvisations I loved in the music of bands like the Grateful Dead were inspired by the modal jams of musicians like Davis and the great saxophonist John Coltrane. Modal music is based more around scales and melodies than chords, and is an approach that's common in traditional music the world over.

Interestingly enough, I learned much later that Pat Martino had never practiced scales, and considered his approach entirely melody-driven. Perhaps if he had been there to teach, he might have gotten through to the derisive jammer.

Another moment that made a great impression on me was at the beginning of an ensemble class. The instructor started off with an experiment: how long could 20-odd guitar players sit with instruments in their hands and not play? Apparently the answer was, not very, and I'm sure that was the outcome the instructor expected. In retrospect, it seems a little absurd that it should have been a challenge—after all, why would someone want to be the first to crack? But crack we did, and that moment remains my strongest memory of that experience.

I remember little else about the music I was supposedly there to study, but the lessons I took away were important ones. I think I didn't learn much about extended jazz harmony because I didn't have the foundation to hear the music in a way that would have made those lessons useful. More to the point, some of my peers at the workshop couldn't hear it either, so they could only "do the math" and plug in the appropriate patterns. This explains the focus on "licks," the need to follow the sheet music, and their difficulty playing simple melody.

COMMUNICATION

I don't mean to make an indictment of jazz or jazz musicians. It's a style I have always admired, and I've come to understand and appreciate it more and more over the years. But its inherent complexity makes it easy for some students to fall into a trap.

The great virtuosos of jazz certainly played fast, intricate, and musically advanced lines when it was called for. But they also understood when to play simply, and how complex parts could be developed from simple foundations. When a group of skilled players does this together, the performance is like a conversation: a discussion and exploration of the ideas presented in the song. In other words, the essence of jazz is not how many notes you play; it's what you play— and how your choices interact with the other players around you. (See Chapter 6, "The Conversation.")

"Copping licks" can be a good thing for a player's learning process, because it's one way we build musical vocabulary. But playing licks can also be like parroting sentences in a language you don't speak. The trap that many of these aficionados had fallen into was that they were learning musical ideas out of context, and so hadn't learned how to make them fit. They were learning the language, and could pronounce the words and use them in a sentence. But they weren't able to break down and develop the ideas themselves yet.

Imagine trying to have a conversation with someone who has only memorized a list of long responses. Someone with a rudimentary vocabulary might only be able to communicate simple ideas, but they can make themselves understood. But an advanced vocabulary out of context is meaningless.

This idea applies in almost any musical setting, not just in jazz. I was about to have that lesson reinforced dramatically and memorably.

IN THE PINES

When I was a teenager, my mother would bring my siblings and me to Pinewoods Camp every summer. Pinewoods was (and still is) a rustic retreat dedicated to traditional New England music and dance. While the adults danced squares and contras in the pavilions, the teens would hang out by the lake and try to sneak beer out of the camp house refrigerator. But I fell in love with the setting, the people, and the music, and returned twice more when I was in college to attend Folk Music Week, one of two weeks in summer dedicated more to music than dancing.

The week following my jazz workshop, I caught a bus from Connecticut to Cape Cod to attend Folk Music Week at Pinewoods, and entered another musical universe. The Gibson and Ibanez "jazz box" guitars were replaced by steel-string Martins, along with fiddles, concertinas, and dulcimers. Most of the attending campers were as accomplished as the faculty leaders, and we spent the week in relaxed workshops on harmony singing, songwriting, fiddle tunes, blues, ancient ballads, and more. We worked in open pavilions or woody smelling cabins. There were concerts every night in the camphouse, followed by impromptu jams. These informal sessions were a striking contrast to my experience the week before.

Many of the aspiring players at the Connecticut workshop I had just left couldn't avoid stepping all over each other, even in groups of two or three. But at folk camp, it wasn't unusual to have twelve musicians sitting in a circle, blending effortlessly on songs they had never played together before. As I joined in the jamming, I also quickly realized that, despite the simplicity of the music, I couldn't match the authority and ease of these more experienced players. As "advanced" as I thought I was, I was working hard to keep up.

I was not new to folk music, having grown up with folk aficionados for parents. I understood the vocabulary, but I had underestimated the difficulty of playing it well. It took me effort and concentration to maintain simple accompaniments that other supposedly less skilled players performed with natural ease. It was an important lesson in the power of simplicity. Playing well has more to do with confidence and authority than with the difficulty of the part.

SETTING A HIGHER STANDARD

There are important reasons to keep stretching your abilities, and that's a big part of practicing. But it's equally important to be able to play something simple with real confidence and authority. Many students and amateurs don't hold themselves to a high enough standard in that respect. Knowing the music well enough to play it through without a mistake is a starting point, not an end. Once you know the notes, you can pay closer attention to style, delivery, and—like the best musicians in any style—really participating in the conversation.

Practicing is not just learning to hit the right notes: it's learning to hit the notes right.

STEALTH MUSICIANSHIP

There are many factors that separate a functional performance from a great one. While you might not always be able to articulate what they are, you will always hear the difference. The subtleties and skill can be easy to miss if nothing flashy or impressive is being played, but if they're absent you'll notice. These finer details of dynamics, timing, and tone are what create "feel," the emotional atmosphere and physical sense of the music.

You might think of music as being abstract, because you can't see it. But all sound is physical, or at least our experience of it is. An object moves in space, creating a change in air pressure that sets off a chain reaction of air molecules bumping into each other. This is the sound wave that reaches your eardrums. These physical fluctuations in air pressure are transformed into electrical impulses, which our brains interpret as sound. So the difference between a great performance and a routine one can literally be something you feel.

I've come to think of this higher level of performance skill as "stealth musicianship," because it almost goes unnoticed. When I was in high school, I played guitar in a jazz band as part of the college prep program for Queens College (where I later went to finish my music degree, as I described in Chapter 3). Our band director Ed Smaldone once gave me a piece of advice about rhythm guitar that I never forgot. He told me that good rhythm guitar should be barely noticeable—but if it wasn't there, "it would leave a hole you could drive a truck through." That might not always be exactly the case, but it's a good thing to keep in mind whenever support and blend matter—meaning, nearly all the time.

It took me a while to take that lesson to heart. As a teenager learning to play music with others, I would sometimes try to make my part "more interesting," usually meaning more complicated. I don't remember being called out for it, but I'm sure it wasn't helping the overall performance. The thing that I didn't yet understand, or wasn't mature enough to appreciate, is how satisfying it is to seamlessly blend into a whole. If you've ever played in an orchestra or wind band, or sang in choir, you understand what that feels like. For a young guitarist fired up by strutting classic rock, it was something I had to learn to appreciate.

But those folk music circles were a powerful reinforcement for my band director's instruction: as the youngest person there, the last thing I wanted was to stand out negatively. I had to concentrate to find something to play that didn't get in the way. This was a good real-world lesson in accompaniment: good supporting parts should be strongly noticeable only if they're missing or outright wrong. Their role is to make the primary voice sound good and add to the overall texture. And the more there is going on, the less each part needs to contribute.

Ultimately, it's not hard to be a good conversationalist: pay attention, and it becomes apparent when to speak, what to say, and when to sit back and listen.

WHAT DOES THIS MEAN TO YOU?

It's absurd to suggest that playing folk music is just as challenging as playing bebop. But the musical dynamics of working in a group are the same in any genre and require similar stealth skills: the ability to listen and react, shaping the music as you play. It's about blending into the ensemble until your part needs to stand out. As a soloist, you'll consciously direct the music in response to the accompaniment and the emotion you feel. The accompaniment can then feed on the energy of the soloist, driving a dynamic feedback loop that makes the music more exciting and powerful.

The best musicians in any genre understand this, and while some vocabularies are more advanced than others, the player must always have a command of the music and the instrument that transcends mere "chops." Great technical skill doesn't automatically mean musicality. Conversely, primitive skills aren't automatically more musical!

The best musicians respond to the demands of the music, whether intuitively or consciously. Sometimes that means playing very simply. And that summer I learned from the folkies at Pinewoods that playing simply is harder than it looks.

THE NEXT STEP

There's no better way to build confidence and authority than to find a situation where you need to deliver the goods. So find a way to prepare for some kind of performance! This might be an open mic at a local venue, a jam session with friends, a video to put on social media, or playing for your dog in the living room. No matter what your musical ambitions and goals might be, getting ready to play for a listener of any kind makes you work through the material on a deeper and more thorough level.

To make this a confidence-building experience rather than a stressful one, choose material that doesn't challenge you too much technically. You need to free yourself to focus on the subtleties, and not be distracted by the effort of playing the notes. It's also an opportunity to appreciate both the challenges and the beauty of well-executed simplicity.

This "performance" doesn't have to be a public presentation on a stage, and while it's great if you can work with a group, it doesn't have to involve other people. Just choose music that you enjoy enough to live with it for a while, and make a commitment to work on it until you feel confident enough to play it in public—even if you never do. Though once you've done this work, you may find yourself wanting to seek an outlet to do just that! It can be helpful—and very satisfying—to have some kind of milestone to give you a sense of completion and accomplishment before you move on to the next set of material.

And above all, recognize that the things that make music memorable have to do with a lot more than the notes you play.

CHAPTER 9

BEGINNER'S MIND

LEARNING
TO PLAY
LIKE A CHILD

We were all beginners once. It might have been when you were a child, or perhaps it was more recently, but your musical journey had to start somewhere. If you think back on what that was like, you might start to remember how differently you saw things from the way you do now. It's more than just having an adult's perspective: the difference has more to do with your own sense of what you can and can't do.

There is a concept in Zen Buddhism called *shoshin*, which translates as "beginner's mind." Beginner's mind could be described as an attitude of openness, eagerness, and lack of preconceptions about a subject, even when working at an advanced level. The beginner is enthusiastic, hungry to learn, and open to possibility. The beginner has yet to experience struggle or failure, and so isn't thinking in terms of what's attainable and what isn't.

This begins to change over time. After a year, or five years, or ten, it's practically impossible not to rate your progress. Now all things are no longer equal: some goals have been attained, others remain out of reach. We note the accomplishments of others and can't help but measure our own against them, not necessarily in a competitive sense, but simply as a yardstick. We form opinions about the relative difficulty of this or that, and about our own potential for meeting the challenge. These opinions can solidify into self-imposed limitations.

A SENSE OF POSSIBILITY

Experience also teaches us to narrow our options, because we've learned what's supposed to work and what isn't. This ability to quickly select the right tool for the job, so to speak, is part of the professional's skill set. But experience can also limit creativity if we stop looking for new approaches in familiar situations. As renowned Zen teacher Shunryu Suzuki wrote in his book *Zen Mind, Beginner's Mind*: "In the beginner's mind there are many possibilities, in the expert's mind there are few."

This is a crucial idea, regardless of how much experience or skill you might have. That sense of possibility is what keeps you motivated, whether that means the possibility of getting better or simply playing with fresh ideas. Since the beginner has no sense of expectation beyond excitement at learning something new, their lack of skill isn't discouraging. Most of all, the beginner has permission to stumble. The experience of playing is satisfying enough when you expect to be able to do it better over time.

Young children, being beginners in everything, exhibit the essence of beginner's mind. Kids learn through play, and they aren't inhibited by whether they know what to do or not. This lack of inhibition, coupled with the lack of experience, encourages creativity and exploration. Kids also don't judge how they spend their playtime as a success or failure—in fact, the idea of such a thing sounds absurd. But as adults, we do this all the time. The collective weight of our knowledge, anxieties, preconceptions, and judgments can be crippling to creativity, motivation, and progress. Cultivating beginner's mind gives you a way out of this trap.

THE CHALLENGE OF THE ADULT BEGINNER

Learning music is supposed to be easiest when you're a child, and many adult students express the wish that they had started earlier. Kids do in fact learn faster than adults, and modern brain science has identified biological reasons why that's the case. But the difference also has a lot to do with the way children learn about the world: through imitation and play. As an adult, you can make a conscious decision to approach your work in a similar way, no matter how old (that is, *experienced*) you are.

Young children's brains do actually have more synaptic connections than those of adults, and consequently a greater degree of neuroplasticity—the ability to form new neural connections. Neuroplasticity decreases with age, but the potential for it never goes away. This is why learning new tasks as an adult helps to keep the mind agile and sharp. The learning process stimulates the formation of new neural connections, even in later adulthood.

Equally important is the fact that the prefrontal cortex, the part of the brain responsible for critical thinking, doesn't develop fully until the mid-20s. This is the reason why young people are more likely to make risky or emotional decisions, rather than thinking from a purely rational perspective. However, the way the prefrontal cortex orders the world also leads to "functional fixedness," in which we see things as what they are rather than what they might be. In other words, a guitar is a guitar and a tennis racket is a tennis racket. But to a child, a tennis racket can be a guitar.

It's not hard to see the impact this has on creativity. Functional fixedness makes "outside the box" thinking much less likely. The more we know about our world, the fewer options we will see in a given situation because of the previous outcomes we've seen. We could choose to simply call this experience, and in many cases the wisdom of experience makes it easier to make good choices. But experience also can lead us to discount the unfamiliar and unusual. The reason you can't teach an old dog new tricks is that he won't recognize it as a new trick. If it has no place in his experience of his world, it doesn't belong and is therefore often ignored.

If you're feeling stuck in your playing, you may not

think a lack of creativity is the issue you're dealing with. But "stuck-ness" (to coin a phrase) is the inability to see other options. Things you have done in the past might have gotten you to where you are, but if they're not helping any more, you need to find a new approach. To do that, you need to be able to imagine what those other paths might be. This requires a level of creativity and open-mindedness that we often lose as we settle into familiar patterns.

MANAGING EXPECTATIONS

All this inspirational talk of childlike play sounds wonderful, until we get to work and realize that we also need structure and focus. The adult student has some real advantages because disciplined focus tends to come more easily with experience. A mindful, targeted approach to any problem is generally the most efficient way to accomplish a task successfully.

So how do we reconcile the need for non-judgmental play with the necessity for time management and thoughtful practice?

First of all, there are different kinds of judgment. There's a big difference between evaluating a single performance versus making broad generalizations about your long-term progress. Focused evaluation is very specific and generally measurable: the goal is usually to hit a specific set of notes at a specific tempo. We identify trouble spots, diagnose problems, and work to find solutions. Since every mechanical problem has a mechanical solution, most challenges can eventually be met with time and repetition.

The problem for most people is not in their ability but in their expectations. A beginner can be shown what and how to practice, and won't expect perfection. That doesn't mean they can't achieve it, but they probably won't have formed an opinion on how much time it will take.

These preconceptions are the single biggest problem most people face; it becomes very difficult to stay motivated in the face of unmet expectations. But since everyone's circumstances are different, it's not realistic to have these expectations in the first place. No one knows what they're capable of when they set out to learn a new skill, but far too many people seem to be solidly convinced of what they aren't capable of.

Self-criticism can be healthy and a great motivator. The issue isn't so much the criticism as much as it is the impact on your desire to do the work. The beginner's non-judgmental perspective allows you to stay focused on small, measurable goals without getting distracted by a running commentary on your overall performance. (For more on effective practice technique, you may want to revisit Chapter 3, "On Practicing.")

EXPLORATION AND DISCOVERY

The other aspect of creativity is, of course, creating—choosing what to play and how to play it. In this area, beginner's mind is possibly the most powerful tool we have. Again, think of a child approaching an instrument for the first time:

the discovery of how it makes a sound, and the delight in exploring it. All kids are capable of this kind of open-ended play, but we often leave that potential behind as we get older. Beginner's mind is the way to get it back.

In 30 years of teaching, I have hardly ever seen someone learn to play well just by practicing the material they were assigned in their lessons. No matter how much instruction you have, players learn by playing. Formal instruction is a great way to develop the mechanics and the vocabulary, but fluid playing requires the ability to make decisions and manipulate notes in the moment. The only way to develop this skill is to do it: to experiment and explore. This is an important part of practicing that some neglect, and it is one of the biggest reasons people get stuck.

Technical practice develops the ability to execute a musical gesture without having to think about it. The notes should just be there when called upon, the way words are there when you want to speak. But practicing "in the moment" is very different from developing technique, because there's no right or wrong way to do it.

If you find it hard to work without specific instructions, you can create open-ended exercises that allow you to explore within particular areas. (The improvisation workshop I described in detail in Chapter 6 was built around this kind of thinking.) By limiting note choices, or even taking pitch completely out of the picture and just working with rhythm, you can manage the problem of "option anxiety." With fewer options, you can simply experiment within a number of finite possible combinations.

In improvising or composing, the challenge for many newcomers is not knowing what to do and feeling inhibited by not wanting to make a mistake. But ultimately, the only mistake is to be so afraid to make one that we become paralyzed.

NON-JUDGMENT

In her excellent book *The Artist's Way*, Julia Cameron talks about starting the day with what she calls "morning pages." This is a freewriting exercise in which you simply write down whatever comes to mind, filling three handwritten pages. It's meant to be a tool for creative exploration, but it's also supposed to develop *non-judgment*. This writing isn't meant to be edited or evaluated in any form. The goal is not to write anything in particular but simply to enter into—and stay in—the stream of consciousness.

Writers often talk about the necessity to separate creating and editing. Many don't correct spelling or grammatical errors when writing drafts, in order to preserve the creative flow. If you've ever taken part in a brainstorming session, you've experienced something similar. In the first stage of brainstorming, there are no bad ideas.

You can approach music the same way, with the added plus that mistakes are gone as soon as the notes fade. So cultivating non-judgment allows you to let mistakes go by without comment or criticism, maintaining the flow state.

Ultimately, this means giving yourself permission to make mistakes. You can address them later when you return to technical practice, but onstage—any stage, formal or informal—is not the time or place. It's essential to make sure any missteps don't linger and snowball into more mistakes as your confidence falters. Your audience will forgive a missed note, but not a tentative performance.

As a musician, you may not always be called upon to create something in the moment. However, every performance should sound as if it was: completely fresh and exciting, no matter how many times you have played the same thing. When you have a lot of history with a song, it's easy to experience it through the lens of all your past performances. But your audience might be hearing it for the first time, and you owe it to them to give them a fully engaged performance. That means being fully present and hearing it as they do: in the moment.

IDEAS FOR EXPLORATION

Whether your goals in music are creative or not, you gain a lot as a player by improvising and exploring:

- **Developing** control of your playing in the moment
- **Deepening** your sensitivity to your musical surroundings
- **Growing** your vocabulary through discovery
- **Bridging** the gaps between idea and execution

- **Connecting** with other musicians through musical conversation
- **Creating** your own voice and repertoire

If you find it challenging to let go and just play, here are some ideas that will help.

1. **Set and setting.** Our own inner critics are judgmental enough. We don't need to give them a reason to comment on what other people might think of your playing. This could mean finding a quiet place to practice out of earshot of others. Perhaps you need headphones or earbuds. Maybe your loved ones should know not to comment on what they might be hearing—unless you ask for feedback. In order to really explore, you must be able to do it without self-consciousness.

2. **Let go of expectations.** This idea has two aspects. One, let go of any expectations of how well you're going to play. Inspiration is fickle. Even great players have days when nothing feels right, and days when they feel like they can do no wrong. Some days you'll be endlessly frustrated, and some days pleasantly surprised. Don't judge: the journey matters more than the destination.

The second aspect is to let go of any preconception of how the music should sound. You may not have any interest in avant-garde freakout jazz, but you might be surprised how interesting ugly and dissonant sounds can be. Non-judgment in this context allows you to explore the full range of what you and your instrument are capable of.

3. **Limit your options.** Limit your musical choices by taking some parameters off the table. For instance, focus on rhythm by playing a melody on a single note. Then try three notes, or five. *Pentatonic scales* are useful for this. When you begin to focus on melody, start off by ignoring rhythm and timing and concentrate on the shape of the line itself: when you go up, when you go down, and by how much.

   Try finding all the different melodic and rhythmic permutations of a small musical idea. Play the same notes at different speeds, starting on different counts, or with varying distances between the notes. Remember that dynamics and tone are musical variables, too. Concentrate on different musical elements at different times: rhythm, melody, harmony (chords), tone, and dynamics. When you focus on one, ignore the others at first, then begin to combine them.

4. **Document and listen.** Record your improvisations and listen to them later. You may surprise yourself! It's a good idea to wait a little while before you listen, though. Waiting until later gives you some distance to hear what you did more clearly (and kindly).

5. **Listen and react.** Once you're comfortable enough with exploring on your own, it's time to start interacting. Many people find it easiest to start with a backing track, or put some music on and just play along. But playing with other musicians should be an ultimate goal, or at least developing the ability to do it.

   This can be tricky, because you need to find people to play with who share a similar mindset, in a situation that allows room for mistakes. Your improvisation can be as simple as learning a couple of pentatonic scales and taking short melodic breaks in the context of a simple song. If the idea of an extended space-jazz opus appeals to you, then by all means pursue it—but it's often best to start simply.

Above all, remember that the ultimate goal here is to be able to *play*, in both senses of the word. Explore with open ears and enjoy the ride.

CHAPTER 10

SKILL, ARTISTRY, & PERSONAL STYLE
THE IMPORTANCE OF BEING YOURSELF

My first guitar teacher, Andy Polon, was a very well-rounded player. He learned to play during the folk boom of the 1960s and had extensive knowledge of folk music and acoustic blues, but he also played jazz and classical guitar and worked those styles into our lessons. He knew I was serious about becoming a musician and wanted to make sure I developed the skills I needed to function as a professional.

I heard other pros say things that reinforced that perspective: if I was going to call myself a guitar player, I needed to have an understanding and a command of different styles of music. The quintessential pro can handle whatever musical language the gig demands, and this was the goal I was aiming for.

When I entered college, my formal studies became more

specific, although my interests remained wide. I became deeply devoted to the classical guitar but played electric guitar in bands on weekends. I started writing songs and learning about recording and production. I wrote solo guitar pieces and played them on recital programs, alongside the compositions of Bach and Villa-Lobos, and I gave a nod to my folkie roots by performing arrangements of traditional melodies.

After graduation, several friends and I made elaborate plans to form a performance collective. We envisioned a dedicated theater and music hall for our collaborative work that would involve musicians, painters, designers, and dancers. I formed a classical trio and wrote and arranged music for us. I also was playing rhythm guitar in a jazz trio, playing solo concerts, and singing folk-rock songs in coffeehouses. It was an exciting and stimulating time.

But classical guitar is ultimately a specialist's domain, too demanding and complex to master with anything less than complete commitment. So while I had completed the path I'd started on when I went to music school, earning a Master's degree in guitar performance, I ultimately left that world behind. (This part of the story is explored in Chapter 7, "The Purist and the Maverick.")

SUSPICIOUS MINDS

I had to rebuild my musical life at 25 after walking away from the classical guitar and recovering from my repetitive strain injury. I had never stopped playing electric and steel-string guitar, and my other musical enthusiasms remained as well. I rededicated myself to writing and singing my own songs, but I also needed to find work.

A year later I was working clubs and restaurants with an oldies band fronted by a youthful but probably fortyish singer whose enthusiasm for Elvis Presley bordered on impersonation. It was a steady gig, but after a year of promises about bigger things and playing "Suspicious Minds" in catering halls, I was ready for something else.

I had also started an acoustic duo with an emphasis on singing harmony. It was 1994, folk-rock was big again, and acts like Indigo Girls and 10,000 Maniacs were filling theaters and were ubiquitous on the radio. After a year of steady gigs performing cover songs, I tried bringing some of my own music to the project. My partner was less than enthusiastic about my material, though, expressing that it didn't "showcase her voice." I didn't fully understand the dynamics of the situation and I thought she was being self-centered.

She may have been, but so was I, and it wasn't inappropriate for either of us. I've come to recognize that an artist *needs* to have a degree of self-centeredness to find and nurture their own voice. I wanted to play my songs the way I heard them, so the natural next step was to lead my own band.

GONE COUNTRY

I formed my own band in 1996 and pulled together a set combining my small repertoire of original songs with a mix of familiar and unfamiliar covers that seemed to fit. At the time, I didn't know I had formed a country band.

It was something of an accident. I remember a specific conversation my wife and I had while walking the dog one night, talking about how all the most successful artists had an identifiable persona and sound. We agreed that I hadn't quite found what that was, but not long after that we found a form of shorthand. I was performing at a neighborhood bar with my acoustic duo one night when my partner's parents came in. The "stage" was just a low platform next to the door, and as they walked by, her father took off the cowboy hat he was wearing and put it on my head. It had never occurred to me to try it before, but the look worked.

I wasn't a fan of country music specifically, and was unfamiliar at the time with the "hat acts" of the early and mid 1990s. But so much of the music I loved was country-influenced: the Rolling Stones, the Eagles, Creedence Clearwater Revival, and the Grateful Dead had all incorporated elements of country music into their sound. The songs I was writing followed that model to some degree, and I was also discovering the folk-influenced Texas sound of progressive country artists like Lyle Lovett and Nanci Griffith. There was also my lifetime love of mountain music from my mother's Kentucky heritage.

To the average Long Island audience, adding the hat to that mix made me a country artist, so I ran with the label and started adding modern country songs to the set. We called the band Jackalope Junction, following an established formula in country of using Western or Southern imagery. We built up to a solid level of local and regional success. But once again I found the label limiting.

LEARNING TO FLY

First of all, there was nothing cool about being country on Long Island. We were too polished and mainstream to fit in with the punk-influenced alt-country movement that was drawing tattooed hipsters to Manhattan venues like the Rodeo Bar. On the other hand, we weren't quite polished *enough* for the gloss of Music Row. There has always been an audience for traditional country in New York, but we didn't really twang either. The local "original music" community was a similarly dubious fit. While there were local country bands that played their own songs, that audience mostly wanted to dance to songs they knew.

Jackalope Junction recorded two albums, both of which did reasonably well for small independent releases. The title track of the second CD *Just Drive* made it into regular rotation on a Nashville radio station and scored a positive review in *Music Row* magazine.

But I was chafing at the country label, having long since ditched the hat, and I wanted to flex different musical muscles. The songs I was writing had taken a different turn. The mood in New York in the years immediately after 9/11 was darker. My music had become more introspective and eclectic, and definitely not right for country radio. Whether I was aware of it at the time, though, I think the shift in direction was also just to prove that I could.

We promoted my first solo CD *Prodigal Son* as an "Americana" release, which made sense for the first song, with its acoustic guitar and fiddle. But the wah-wah guitar in the next song started to pull things in another direction, and by the time track 6 introduced a classical guitar, the "genre" question had become difficult to answer. I remember being told by a label representative that he loved the CD and that it hadn't left his truck, but that the company couldn't do anything with it because "we do Americana music."

That particular genre definition is still hazy, and you might be hard pressed to really pin down what it is. "Roots music" might hit closer to the mark. But either way, there was nothing "roots" about the album's final track, a nylon-string guitar instrumental with layers of cello and violin. Once again, I had managed to incorporate elements of a genre while not exactly fitting into it.

The next project complicated matters still further. I had secured an endorsement with Parker Guitars, a small company that made high-tech, cutting-edge boutique instruments. With its incredibly thin body, light weight, and big sound, the Parker Fly was a very comfortable guitar to play—especially when my repetitive strain problems acted up. Wanting to make the most of the endorsement, I pitched the company the idea of recording a project that featured Parker instruments exclusively, thinking that it could be a great cross-promotional tool. They loved the idea and loaned me several guitars to use for the album, called (of course) *Flying*.

The album did well enough to earn a distribution deal, and it helped to establish me as the kind of player I wanted to be seen as. But from the perspective of developing a creative career, a diverse instrumental not-quite-jazz project was another stylistic hard left turn. My high-tech instrument also wasn't right for the "roots" label I had been trying to cultivate.

I was starting to run up against what I now see as an inescapable fact: that while my training prepared me well for a career as a versatile working musician, my versatility was making it difficult to develop the kind of singular voice I needed as an artist.

THE ARTIST'S VOICE

Musicians develop their style by absorbing the sound of their inspirations and mentors. Some learn to be effective mimics, while others become individuals. Some develop a deep knowledge of the nuances of a style, while others bring a vision and personality strong enough to create their own.

When I was first learning to play, all my musical heroes had a singular style you could easily recognize. Musical personalities come across in a variety of ways, all reflecting the player's influences and choices, conscious and unconscious. This impacts everything from the way they physically approach their playing to their phrasing, note choices, and preferred type of instrument. The combined effect of all these factors creates an identifiable, personal sound.

But most formal training actually points in the opposite direction. A good portion of my musical life had centered on imitating and reproducing familiar sounds. You could probably say the same for most people who have studied formally in any setting. That formal education is meant to build the basic skills you need to play any style of music. You can choose to focus on a particular genre or specialty, but a professional player doesn't always know what the next gig will be and therefore must function in a variety of musical settings.

You could think of this philosophy as a "liberal arts" model of music: regardless of where you might land professionally, a well-rounded education is the best preparation. This is certainly true for the freelancer and pro side player, and as a gigging musician that background kept me working. Rock, blues, jazz, country, folk, classical—whatever the gig called for, I needed to be prepared for it. When I was devouring the pages of *Guitar Player* magazine as a teenager, I read every article and every lesson column, whether I understood it or not, and I resolved to learn more if I didn't. My goal was to be the best and most versatile musician I could be.

An artist doesn't share the same imperatives as a working pro player, however. A performing artist needs a distinctive style and sound to stand out, and the most successful are often the most strikingly original. When

I look back at the musicians who had the biggest impact on me as a player, you could say that about virtually all of them. Pioneering Latin rock guitarist Carlos Santana once said in an interview, "Your tone is your face. Why would you want to look like someone else?"

Like most people, I started out as a student and a fan first, learning by imitating my heroes. They taught me what was possible, expanding my concept of what a guitar could do, and I built my vocabulary by stealing from them all. But while many of these players were and are great masters of their instrument, they were not chameleons. They may have started off as I did, imitating their inspirations, but they eventually began to stake out territory of their own.

This process is partly just a matter of absorbing and internalizing influences, but there's another crucial element. Style is also shaped by our limitations, and the choice whether to overcome or to incorporate them.

On a very basic level, this comes up all the time, both in my own playing and in lessons with my students. For example, it's often possible to find workarounds or make small changes to make a challenging part easier to play. For the student, this can be a cop-out. After all, without challenge we don't grow. But for the performer who can play the song without difficulty except for one particular change or passage, that one small roadblock can make the difference between being able to perform the song or not. If that's the case, I'll often choose or suggest the workaround. The skill development question can often be addressed in some other way. In the case of the performing artist who simply wants to be expressive, one solution might be as good as another if it creates the desired effect. There can be multiple ways to create a particular feeling.

WHAT DOES THIS MEAN TO YOU?

Developing an individual style may not be a high priority for the average student or hobbyist. Learning to play favorite songs is satisfying enough for many people. But even if your musical tastes as a listener are diverse, you might find that you have a musical "home base" that you return to, even as you explore different sounds. So style is defined by musical preference and genre, as well as your own aesthetic sensibility. We all gravitate towards sounds we find pleasing and compelling.

The finer technical points of style develop over time. Every aspect of your technique has an impact on your sound, including the way you breathe and carry your body. (See Chapter 4, "Instrument and Body.") So even if you're not consciously trying to be an individual, you already are. When you start to recognize this, you are faced with an important choice: how much do you allow your predispositions to shape your style, and how much do you consciously try to absorb things you admire in other players?

This is not always a conscious decision. Intuitive players are naturally guided by what they hear and find pleasing, so individual style tends to develop on its own. Players who choose to develop more wide-ranging skills are also choosing to have more control over their options. With more control and a larger vocabulary, a player's style can change according to the demands of the music. This is a requirement for the professional session player and most working musicians in general.

For a creative artist, though, this kind of versatility has a downside. Style can be a product of the player's physical approach to the instrument—touch, attack, and energy—as well as their musical choices. So in this sense, it's inherent. But a distinctive voice can be obscured by stylistic "masks." Again, this may be a conscious choice if the player is called upon to reproduce a sound. But for the most distinctive artists, style comes through in any musical setting.

You may not have begun to develop a style and "sound" of your own. As you continue to learn, though, you will find that some things come more naturally than others. Don't shy away from the challenges—they will help you grow! But start to recognize your musical "home" and get to know that territory as well as you can. There's always more you can do to develop your style with confidence and authority. You might find yourself gravitating to a certain style of playing. Explore the nuances that make the great players sound the way they do.

If you're still a beginner or a long-term beginner, this process may not have begun yet. But the more you play and the better you listen, the more you'll find a sound starting to take shape. When that begins to happen, embrace it and dive in deeper. Sometimes that means working with and around your limitations, but that won't stop you from growing. What it will do is allow you to grow as an artist, not just as a player.

CHAPTER 11

STUCK
TEACHER,
TEACH THYSELF

One of the great challenges of presenting yourself to the world as an authority is that you're expected to have answers. Fortunately, my personal and professional history as a student, performer, and teacher has given me the means to help my students find the answers they need. I certainly hope this book bears that out.

However, we are all only human and prone to falling into the same traps. My ability to write this book hasn't made me immune to the challenges of improving as a musician. Like you, I have struggled with frustration and boredom. For every performance where it seemed I could do no wrong, there were five more that were full of missteps, mistakes, and uninspired moments. Fortunately, the professional learns to recover quickly when things go wrong, and most mistakes go unnoticed by much of the audience. And just as a comic can keep the crowd on his side even when he's not going over by making a joke of it, a spectacular fail onstage can be forgivably entertaining.

Pros can deliver a strong performance whether they're feeling inspired or not. In fact, the defining quality of a professional is that ability to come through consistently, regardless of the circumstances. However, there's no denying that when the performer is feeling inspired, the performance is elevated to another level. So accessing inspiration is a constant goal for every artist. But while writing this book, I went through a period when I found it difficult.

I had left the performing project I had been devoting most of my efforts to so I could free up time to work on the book and make new music of my own. I didn't know what that new music was going to sound like, though. Without a commitment to an established project, I had no imperative to play in a particular style. It felt like a good time to just explore and let the music find its own way.

This should have been a satisfying place to be. One of the nice things about wrapping up a project is the freedom to explore again. I remember feeling the same way in school after playing a recital program I'd spent months preparing. A diverse skill set keeps many options open, as we explored in Chapter 10, and I was excited by the prospect of something new.

But the next thing didn't reveal itself easily, and I found

myself feeling stuck. Everything I played seemed tired and overly familiar. It was easy enough to go through the motions and deliver a solid performance, but the joy and inspiration weren't there. It was as if I had run out of ideas; I was tired of everything I knew how to do, but unable to find something more stimulating. Ironically enough, I was writing a book about how to stay musically connected but I had become disconnected myself.

But this situation also presented an unexpected opportunity. What better way to illustrate the process of getting "unstuck" than to go through it myself and then share the story?

CHOICES

Everyone's musical journey is a series of choices. Writing a song or improvising a solo requires a series of choices, and each one determines the options for the next. In beginning to observe my own situation, the first thing I noticed was that I wasn't choosing as consciously as I could.

One of the driving concepts of "beginner's mind" is that the beginner's lack of knowledge is actually an asset to creativity (as was discussed in Chapter 9). Everything is new and unknown, so one option is just as possible as another. The expert, on the other hand, is usually in familiar territory. Experience produces a hierarchy of possibilities, from most common to least. The expert player has a variety of options immediately available, based on experience of what has worked in the past.

For the last several years, I've had a steady monthly gig at a small venue just outside Nashville. It's a very loose situation; I can play pretty much whatever I like for an audience that's generally receptive to whatever we choose to do. The set list usually includes a number of blues standards, some of which I've played regularly for 30 years. This is very familiar territory. Midway through a tune one night, I suddenly realized that I was playing automatically. It's not that the music lacked feeling, but the paths I was choosing were so well worn that the notes practically played themselves.

This might sound like a good thing, until you realize that there's a difference between not having to think about what you're playing and just *not thinking*. In other words, going with the flow was taking me down the path of least resistance every time. There was nothing wrong with the note choices themselves. But the gestures were automatic and had become repetitive. No wonder I was bored with my playing. I had stopped looking for different possibilities.

NOT-DOING

There is a concept in Chinese philosophy of *wu-wei*, or "not-doing." The literal translation is something like "without exertion." We might think of it as another way of describing a flow state, of being "in the zone"—performing an action or activity effortlessly. This is the state we ultimately aspire to when playing.

Part of the long-term effect of repetitive practice is to reinforce an action to the point where its execution doesn't require anything more than the intent to do it. However, the actions need to be driven by ideas. Sometimes—rarely—we find a flow of pure inspiration, and the magic just happens. But music is made up of patterns and we are creatures of habit. This can lead to exactly the kind of repetition that was leaving me uninspired. Having the ability to play without thinking doesn't mean you always should.

But on this particular night, I found a way to direct the flow and practice "not-doing" at the same time. I began to ask myself a simple question: what else could I do here? In practice, this meant hesitating a moment more before starting to play, pausing just long enough to avoid automatically plugging in the most familiar thing. But the fascinating part is that I didn't choose to do anything in particular. Rather, I chose not to do the first thing that came to mind. The effect was dramatic, and I found myself immediately playing with much more creativity and spark. Playing well is a feedback loop: inspiration breeds more inspiration. When you play something you really like, it makes you want to keep playing to see what will happen next.

The "aha" moment here was that I didn't need to go looking for something specific to play. I simply chose not to follow the first impulse that arose and see what the alternatives would be. Sometimes it did involve a little more direction, but only in a general sense: go down instead of up, shift to a new position, or change the scale. This kept the spontaneous flow open. My directions were broad enough to leave room for multiple options at any given moment.

THE BREAKDOWN

Of course, this is the culmination of a process. My accumulated experience and knowledge of music provided the background. I needed to have a vocabulary of musical choices I knew I could make, and the technical ability to spontaneously play things I hadn't specifically practiced. Even something as simple as choosing to use a different finger to play a particular note demands a level of control. So there was a great deal of time and effort behind the spontaneity, in that I was working with elements that had been already prepared.

One of the larger threads throughout this book is the idea that music is made up of concrete elements that can be identified, categorized, and manipulated. This breaks down to a lot of information, but it also gives you a natural way to organize your practice. Working through it all takes time, and I was fortunate enough to have that luxury when I was a music student and my primary responsibility was to do just that. Most people don't have that kind of time to devote to practicing, but an organized long-term strategy will help you make the most of the time you do have. (See Chapter 3, "On Practicing.")

My students are sometimes surprised by how far we break things down in their lessons. But I don't think most people break things down far enough. (For that matter, we could say the same thing about many teachers.) Most people learn to memorize and execute parts, and they eventually develop a large enough vocabulary of parts to play a variety of songs. But an essential long-term goal should be to develop a larger facility, not just on the instrument, but also with musical ideas. A good musician should be able to experiment with different *sounds* in a conscious way. Facility with the elements of music will give you choices, while skill on the instrument will provide the means to execute them.

DO SOMETHING

These musical choices don't even have to involve the notes. When I was a student at the Manhattan School, my guitar teacher Nicholas Goluses and I had a conversation one day about technique. He said it was important to remember that all musical gestures require some kind of change in how you approach the instrument, and that all those changes fall into the category of technique. Many people think of technique strictly in terms of speed and a high degree of quick dexterity. This is all true, but highly technical patterns are still just musical gestures, none more important than any other. There are many subtle ways to affect the sound of a note, and they all involve a level of command of the instrument.

Later on during the same lesson, Nick was coaching me through a piece. When a particular passage wasn't working, he stopped me and asked me to play a segment. As I did, he would simply say, "Do something." He meant "make a musical decision" and I did. A moment later he said it again and I responded. This was a composed piece and I didn't have the option of changing the notes. But I could experiment with the dynamics: the rise and fall in volume and energy. So in response to his cues, I tried shaping the line according to the way I felt the music unfolding. The performance immediately became much more fluid and musical, and most importantly, it had more conviction and feeling.

The choices were broad gestures, and of course, the command "do something" is about as broad as you can get. But because I had practiced working with many different aspects of music as individual parts, the options were familiar and readily available. This familiarity is what makes it possible to have command of the different elements in real time, and to allow some of that play to happen intuitively.

It might sound overly simplistic to say that the solution to feeling stuck is to do something different. But taken in the broadest sense, that is ultimately how we solve any problem when our regular approaches don't work. Remember the old saw about the definition of insanity as doing the same thing repeatedly and expecting a different result? There are many things you could choose to do differently in response to the simple command to "do something." We should also add another word: do something else.

SOMETHING ELSE

During this recent "stuck" period, I had a conversation with a friend—a musician and producer and one of the most highly creative people I know. I had reached out to him to ask for his perspective on getting out of my own rut. His response was, "Maybe you should make a record without any guitar on it?"

This was an interesting suggestion. There's no better way to break out of familiar patterns than to move into a situation where the old patterns won't work. I've played piano most of my life, so I do have some facility with that instrument—not nearly to the degree I do on guitar, but comfortably enough to play piano on my own recordings. I wasn't about to commit myself to a project, but I did like the idea of stepping away from the guitar for a bit.

I have automatic patterns on piano just as I do on guitar, however. And I've observed that it's not only my fingers that settle into patterns—my mind does, too. I've found myself playing with similar musical ideas on either instrument. That's not a bad thing, because it means that I'm playing what I hear rather than being led by my fingers. But those patterns can become locked in as well.

Fortunately, the piano is a great instrument to explore on. Once your basic technique is in place, it's not significantly harder to play in one key than in another. I also find the tactile sense of the piano very satisfying, in the way the keys and the sound will respond to variations in touch. In fact, you can treat the keyboard like a drum: just choose a set of notes and a pattern of left- and right-hand beats. So I could begin by settling into a groove and vamping on a single chord or pattern. It felt good to just lay into something simple, and before long things began to open up.

I alternated between free improvisation and working from music. I kept my dog-eared *Real Book* on the piano (see Chapter 8, "Simplicity and Authority") and learned tunes. Often the song would spin off into a new improvisation, sometimes following the chord structure of the tune and sometimes not. At other times, I just let my fingers fall, not worrying about what sounds were going to come out. I tried to just enjoy the sound and feel of the piano, and let the rest unfold as it would.

FULL CIRCLE

As I continued to explore on the piano, I was also getting back to songwriting, something I hadn't spent much time on for several years. I've never been a very prolific writer. I tend to write a handful of songs a year, and I spend weeks and even months trying out different arrangement possibilities. But I recognized I needed a shot in the arm, and getting back to co-writing was also a great way to reconnect with people I hadn't seen in a while.

My explorations on piano weren't necessarily carrying over into these co-writing sessions. The songs that emerged were simple and straightforward, but I felt better about the new material than I had about any collection of music in a long time. By throwing the door wide open and allowing myself to go anywhere in my exploratory practice, I had reconnected emotionally with things that were most familiar and comfortable. Rather than feeling like the ideas were tired, I felt like I had come home.

As I write this today, I'm enjoying playing music once again. I've been through this cycle before, and I'll go through it again. But the fact that I was working on this book during this time gave me a different perspective and made the process that much more conscious. I can see I applied many of the big ideas we've explored throughout this book:

1. Applying beginner's mind at the piano (Chapters 6 and 9)
2. Reconnecting with my musical roots and peers (Chapters 1 and 8)
3. Improvising and choosing to explore (Chapter 6)
4. Checking in with my body and physical sense of the instrument (Chapter 4)
5. Listening for and finding new musical connections (Chapter 5)

The most important factors were—and are—at the heart of the message of this book:

- We seek connection through music, and we remain open and motivated by approaching the task with a beginner's mind.

- Ultimately we play music to connect to ourselves, to the people we play with, and to the people listening.
- Nothing makes you relax into playing better than the pure joy of doing it when it feels right.
- "Right" is a product of preparation and inspiration.
- Above all, the love of music encourages the work and cultivates love in return.

CREDITS & ACKNOWLEDGEMENTS

So many people played a part in the creation of this book that there's no way to thank them all. I've learned as much from my students and colleagues as I did from my teachers, in fact I continue to. All of these people collectively helped form my philosophy and approach as a musician and educator. So this is by necessity an incomplete list, but the names to follow are some the people that had the most direct impact on me - and this book itself.

My parents brought me up in a house full of music, and taught me to love it. Some of my earliest musical memories are of my mother playing Bartok on the piano and singing folk songs to me, and the sound of my father's guitar and recordings of Doc Watson and Segovia.

My guitar teachers Andy Polon, Alan Spriestersbach, Benjamin Verdery, Nicholas Goluses, and Mark Delpriora helped me discover what I was capable of as a player. Edward Smaldone gave me my first lessons in ensemble skills in the jazz band at the Aaron Copland School of Music preparatory division when I was in high school. Every one of my professors throughout my academic career made an impact, but I want to give special mention to the courses I took with Bruce Saylor and Charles Burkhart at the Copland School and with David Noon and Nils Vigeland at the Manhattan School Of Music.

There's no way for me to name all the musicians I've worked with, you've all made an impact one way or another. Some of you became and will remain family – you know who you are.

In Nashville, Kim Copeland and Susan Tucker got me started writing about music and creativity in 2009 by inviting me to write for their Songwriters Connection blog, beginning the creative process that culminates in these pages as well as a friendship and professional relationship that continues to this day.

My relationship with the Nashville Songwriters Association International (NSAI) over the past fifteen years has similarly been invaluable for developing and refining these ideas, thanks in no small part to NSAI Executive Director Bart Herbison's belief in my teaching.

I am deeply indebted to Maryglenn McCombs and Dan Chiras for their guidance and encouragement through this entire process. That first lunch we had together made me feel that I was ready to write this book. Special thanks as well to Mary Sack for sharing her expertise and vast network to point me towards the people I needed to complete the picture.

My wife Jeri's unwavering love, belief in my abilities, and insight have made every career accomplishment over the last twenty-five years possible, and helped me discover what I'm capable of as a person.

Dave Isaacs
Nashville, TN
July 1, 2019

Editing: Mary Helen Clarke, Andy Ellis
Artwork and design: Christa Schoenbrodt, Studio Haus
Author photo credit: Andy Ellis

Special thanks: John and Kate Richardson at InDo Nashville, Bonnie St. Martin, Laura Rabell, Christopher Geiersbach, Tim Morgan, Andrea Robertson, Linda Chiras, Scott Davidson, Hank Ingram, and Richard Courtney.

ABOUT THE AUTHOR

Musician and educator Dave Isaacs has called Nashville home since 2005, where he has built a reputation as an ace guitarist and top teacher and mentor to aspiring and professional musicians, songwriters, and performing artists. Dave holds a Master of Music degree from the Manhattan School of Music in New York and has taught music to students of all ages and skill levels, in private lessons, workshops, and college classrooms. He has been a music instructor at Tennessee State University and the Art Institute of Tennessee – Nashville, and now maintains a thriving private teaching studio and speaking schedule. He is also active as a performer, songwriter, and recording artist. "The Perpetual Beginner" is his first book.

PRAISE FOR DAVE ISAACS

"Dave Isaacs is an outstanding teacher because he is part fan, part musician, part songwriter, part psychologist and part motivator. You won't even be finished with the first chapter of his book when this will be apparent. Dave manages to take all those things and weave them into a must-read work that will benefit, challenge and inspire you."

- BART HERBISON, EXECUTIVE DIRECTOR
  NASHVILLE SONGWRITERS ASSOCIATION
  INTERNATIONAL (NSAI)

"Dave Isaacs has captured what it takes to 'create' music and become a more, better accomplished 'musician' while continuing to hone the craft. I think this is going to be a great read for actual beginners, as well as, the 'perpetual' beginner."

- KAREN E. REYNOLDS, EAST TENNESSEE WRITERS HALL
  OF FAME SINGER SONGWRITER | MUSIC INDUSTRY
  CONSULTANT

"Dave Isaacs provides an interesting reveal on the history of his musical journey. The story includes personal, philosophical, musical, and historical, perspectives on not just mastering an instrument, but how music can be perceived and used as a surprisingly nuanced form of communication. "The Perpetual Beginner" is conceived and written from a wonderful point of view that offers a different perspective on what it means to be a musician."

- RICHARD ADLER, GRAMMY-WINNING PRODUCER AND ENGINEER

"Dave is right on the money. Follow his advice and you will become a better player!"

- GARY TALLEY, MEMPHIS MUSIC HALL OF FAME SONGWRITER AND LEAD GUITARIST FOR THE BOX TOPS

Some guitarists are gifted players and a few guitarists are gifted teachers, but it's rare to find someone who has full command of both disciplines. Dave Isaacs is one such musician, and in this book he distills a lifetime of study, performing, and instruction into inspiring, practical advice that will benefit beginners and seasoned professionals alike.

—ANDY ELLIS, FORMER SENIOR EDITOR, *GUITAR PLAYER* MAGAZINE

CPSIA information can be obtained
at www.ICGtesting.com
Printed in the USA
LVHW111949270919
632500LV00003B/558/P